THE FOG OF REFORM

Other Books by George A. Goens

Resilient Leadership for Turbulent Times: A Guide to Thriving in the Face of Adversity
Soft Leadership for Hard Times
Straitjacket: How Overregulation Stifles Creativity and Innovation in Education

THE FOG OF REFORM

Getting Back to a Place Called School

George A. Goens

ROWMAN & LITTLEFIELD
Lanham • Boulder • New York • London

Published by Rowman & Littlefield
A wholly owned subsidiary of The Rowman & Littlefield Publishing Group, Inc.
4501 Forbes Boulevard, Suite 200, Lanham, Maryland 20706
www.rowman.com

Unit A, Whitacre Mews, 26-34 Stannary Street, London SE11 4AB

Copyright © 2016 by Rowman & Littlefield

All rights reserved. No part of this book may be reproduced in any form or by any electronic or mechanical means, including information storage and retrieval systems, without written permission from the publisher, except by a reviewer who may quote passages in a review.

British Library Cataloguing in Publication Information Available

Library of Congress Cataloging-in-Publication Data

Names: Goens, George A.
Title: The fog of reform : getting back to a place called school / George A. Goens.
Description: Lanham, Maryland : Rowman & Littlefield, [2016] | Includes bibliographical references and index.
Identifiers: LCCN 2015048431 (print) | LCCN 2016002351 (ebook) | ISBN 9781475826968 (cloth : alk. paper) | ISBN 9781475826975 (pbk. : alk. paper) | ISBN 9781475826982 (electronic)
Subjects: LCSH: School improvement programs–United States. | Educational change–United States. | Public schools–United States–Evaluation. | Education–Aims and objectives–United States.
Classification: LCC LB2822.82 .G59 2016 (print) | LCC LB2822.82 (ebook) | DDC 371.2/07–dc23
LC record available at http://lccn.loc.gov/2015048431

∞ ™ The paper used in this publication meets the minimum requirements of American National Standard for Information Sciences Permanence of Paper for Printed Library Materials, ANSI/NISO Z39.48-1992.

Printed in the United States of America

For My Father
He died when I was four years old. His absence was present throughout my life. I miss him to this day.

※ ※ ※

For My Mother
She instilled in me the importance of teachers and hard work.

※ ※ ※

For Marilyn
"Do you believe in miracles?" Her presence in my life is just that.

CONTENTS

Preface: An Inside Look ... ix
Introduction ... xv

PART I: THE FOG ... 1
1 The Fog of Reform ... 3
2 Fog and Ethical Pitfalls ... 13
3 Assumptions, Evaluation, and Carrots and Sticks ... 27

PART II: LIFTING THE FOG ... 39
4 The Foundation: Public Education ... 41
5 Education or Schooling? ... 53
6 What Is an Educated Person? ... 61
7 Leadership and Accountability ... 73
8 Polestars, Parents, and Pupils ... 85
9 The Soul of Schools ... 99

PART III: WHAT WE MUST DO ... 107
10 Moral Imperative ... 109
11 What We Must Do ... 123
12 The Fog of Reform: Lessons ... 133

Bibliography ... 145
Index ... 149

About the Author 153

PREFACE

An Inside Look

When you listen to pundits, talking heads, and school reformers, you would guess that schools are about organizational structure, inputs and outputs, data points, union contracts, test scores, and markets. How things change. In the discourse and debate, claims are made and so-called data are presented. Although special and corporate interests are promoted, we overlook students.

We seldom asked them what they want school to be and what they want from teachers. Too often we look at students as objects, statistics, or "customers." Maybe our children have insight into what schools are and what they should be, and maybe that insight can lead us out of the fog of reform.

So in researching and writing this book, I asked a 15-year-old high school student to write an essay, without adult influence or editing, about her perspective on schools and teachers. As of this writing, Claire Bower lives in Florida and is a sophomore in a suburban high school. This is what Claire wrote:

> What school is, and what school should be, is a topic that is often debated in modern days by politicians, parents, educators, and students. School should be a place of learning, a safe haven for creativity, originality, and innovation where the next generation has the opportunity to grow and form new ideas. Although, nowadays students often feel limited and constrained by school as it has evolved

over the years into a monstrous system of testing and standardization which limits their potential and induces stress and discouragement.

Classrooms should be a place where students are free to express their ideas and opinions. Teachers should encourage new ideas and concepts, they should show pupils that they are all valued individuals and support students' educational endeavors, showing that they genuinely care. School has become diluted, not fully fulfilling its purpose of teaching and inspiring the next generation of innovators and creators. This must be changed as teachers and schools have extremely important roles, and impact students' upbringing, character, and outlook more than many realize.

First and foremost teachers have the opportunity to impact students' lives. I know from personal experience that teachers have the power to influence their students' outlooks positively or negatively and it's up to the teachers to accept their jobs and choose what type of impact they will have. Making a positive impact includes being a compassionate and kind person who displays a genuine interest in students' lives. Showing students that they matter is essential, when people feel accepted, supported, and valued they will be motivated to do work and put forth effort. If students are not shown their importance they will feel as if they are just another pupil in just another class and will be less driven to participate and reach out to have a communicative, healthy student-teacher relationship in which support and learning is bred.

What happens to teachers, or anyone, when they feel ignored, disrespected, or unappreciated? Naturally they become frustrated and change their attitudes. This, too happens to students. Students will become agitated with a class and/or teacher and lack effort and motivation if they feel ignored or set aside. If children are made to be just another test score and feel limited and defined by their tests, homework assignments, and knowledge gained throughout the year, they will become frustrated with school and lose interest and inspiration. It is vital that each and every student is shown their importance so that they will feel driven and be propelled to reach their potential.

Uniqueness should be encouraged and individuality should be embraced, it is critical that all those involved in the education system recognize that every child is different, every student learns differently, and it is the innovators and those who challenge what the world already knows that start revolutions. Therefore, teachers need to understand it is not only their job to teach facts and give lectures, it is also their job to support students, offer advice, and have an open mind to new ideas and concepts.

Just as teachers have an obligation to attempt to positively impact students, school as a whole also has a job. The purpose of school is to teach students, and students attend school to learn. In my opinion, and in the opinion of many of my fellow peers, school has lost its meaning.

School has transformed into a focused machine, which gives standardized tests and discourages any form of unique self-expression. In English, the standard is that all papers must be formatted and structured the same; in history, the curriculum only presents the standard one-sided American perspective when looking at the motives of historical wars; when taking a standardized reading comprehension test if you have a different opinion or interpretation of the piece than the "correct" answer you are all of a sudden entirely wrong . . . and I present the question of "why?" to you.

Why has our country's education system lost its focus on teaching and instead taken up such a standardized mentality, with the main premise of this standardized concept being testing. School was made for teaching, not testing; and that is how it should be today. Granted some tests are necessary to determine the effectiveness of a teacher and/or curriculum, but the amount of standardized testing in today's schools is absolutely absurd. All year children hear "The test at the end of the year," "On your EOC [end-of-course exam]," "Remember for your test," "To pass the test," etc. Quite frankly these tests may be called standardized but in reality they aren't.

Now I must make myself clear when addressing this topic and state that I do believe the teachers are not at fault when it comes to the standardized tests. Teachers are not the ones mandating that students take these tests; in fact teachers suffer along with the students. Teachers must struggle to readjust the curriculum to ensure they prepare students for the state mandated exams.

Tests truly put a damper on classroom productivity. There is no doubt that these standardized tests imposed by the government negatively impact both students and teachers.

Every teacher teaches differently, every student learns differently, in every classroom different information is taught and at different speeds, so how are these tests given statewide considered "standardized" when every classroom is different?

Furthermore, much of the school year teachers have to give up valuable teaching time so that students can go through standard preparation procedures for these tests and for the tests in general. This time that students spend sitting and answering multiple-choice questions for the tests is time that could be spent in the classroom learning. Students gain nothing from the tests except stress and lack of classroom learning time, so really they gain nothing at all.

School is about teaching students, school is about students, so why is there such a focus on something that doesn't benefit the students and why are millions of dollars a year spent on these tests? Instead the money spent on these tests could be going toward schools so that programs could be better and children would have even more opportunities to learn. The government needs to allow schools to readjust their focus and get back to the roots of the education system in which there was minimal testing and an objective to teach students in the best way possible, for their benefit and not for the achievement of high "standardized" test scores.

Not only do these tests affect students' learning, they also impact students' attitudes and the effort they put in towards school. These standardized tests make children feel as if they are just another test score, and just another part of the system. They communicate to a student that as long as they can pass the end of the year exams for their courses that's all that matters.

The whole school year should not be focused on these tests, which don't present themselves till the latter part of the year. Students should be working and striving for greatness throughout the entire school year with the help of their teachers. Teachers should be allowed to make an effort to teach relevant information in interesting ways which engage students, although often times this can't be done due to the many regulations and rules placed upon them.

On another note, teachers should also be aware of how each of their different classes and students learn best so that they may communicate to each class as well as possible. If teachers are making an effort to engage students, incorporate creative activities, and build lesson plans around how they think their class will learn best, students will be more apt to put in effort in return.

Yes, of course, there will always be those students who lack any kind of drive or motivation and who will be non-participatory, but the students who are willing to work and have the yearning to succeed will do so with the help of their teachers. Not only will this help teachers motivate students more and make class more interesting, it will also help students gather and retain information better as they will be increasingly capable of remembering specific details due to the fact that they found certain activities and lessons intriguing.

Teachers should have the power to make class more engaging, motivational and inspiring for students who do have potential and do want to learn. It is crucial that teachers have the opportunity to do so; motivated students are working students, working students are innovative students, and innovation will lead to a bright future for themselves and the international community as a whole.

School is a privilege and there are many areas of the world in which it is rare for children to receive an education. With this in mind, those who have the blessing of receiving an education should appreciate it immensely and those working to educate the youth should take their job seriously and do it to the best of their ability.

The education system must get back to teaching children for the pure cause of their learning. Society must not over complicate the system by implementing a multitude of standardized tests which realistically only take away from the teaching and learning which is the primary goal.

Children must feel like they are more than test scores and should be shown compassion, kindness, and care by school faculty; their ideas must be considered with open minds, as much of the youth today have refreshing, eye opening opinions which should be taken seriously and could positively impact the world. Moreover, students must be able to express themselves, explore new concepts, and challenge common beliefs and widely accepted theories.

For we must keep in mind that some of the greatest discoveries throughout history have come from people who were willing to take a chance and go after something, even if they didn't know what the outcome would be. That is exactly why the education system must not put the youth in a creativity constraining box, but instead schools should be "boxes" in which creativity is encouraged and allowed to flourish. The schools in the United States and around the world should work to encourage, lift up, motivate, inspire, and teach the next generation of innovators, creators, artists and geniuses; it is vitally important that work is done so that schools can do just that.

Claire's viewpoint as a student differs from what many reformers advocate. She looks at it from the perspective of a student with ten years of experience. Her view is compassionate toward teachers and fellow students but not very optimistic about her experiences in a "standardized" environment. All of us need places of understanding, care, and nurturing, no matter what our age.

Today, reforms have turned many schools into pressure cookers—harried and intense places—with technology and assessments at center stage. Claire and her fellow students deserve far more than that.

Claire A. Bower is a 15-year-old sophomore in high school in Florida. She is interested in the arts and is involved in theater, music, writing, journalism, and other activities. She plans to attend college and pursue studies in theater, public relations, and journalism.

INTRODUCTION

One question seems to go unanswered when it comes to school reform. Actually, it is the essential question behind any effort to change or improve schools. Simply put, what is a place called school? Determining what schools are raises many questions—both philosophical and practical.

Historically from Sputnik and A Nation at Risk to No Child Left Behind and Race to the Top, politicians and others have pushed for school reform. A profusion of proposals and books have been published, each diagnosing problems and making recommendations. Many are naive, fragmented, or detached from the complex realities of school. Some are the product of special interests that stand to profit from them.

Articles, commentators, and even Hollywood have proclaimed that public education is sick, if not dead, and that the answers are to be found in market-driven competition, testing, and technology, along with firing teachers, eliminating unions, and supporting charter schools or for-profit ventures. Critics, who have neither toiled nor experienced the real day-to-day life of schools, have prospered from pitching their solutions in books and the media. But simplistic platitudes such as "choice" and "vouchers" or "data-based decision making" are off the mark and miss the true work of schools.

The compelling motive behind most of these initiatives is to find a "cure" for schools. These "magic bullet" or "quick-fix" remedies create a sense of meaninglessness and indifference in the minds of many educators as waves of new fads wash over the schools. Teachers yearn for substance to help the children that come to them, not for top-down systems, "data mining," and test-driven cultures. Data may be a tool, but unless it is accurate, applied meaningfully, and linked to noble ideals, it is an irrelevant distraction.

A fog of reform is created obscuring issues and deflecting our focus from the real mission of schools. We need to emphasize ideals and principles in providing an education for our children in a caring and creative way. In the attempt to reach these ideals, schools become better.

Madness is the dissonance between metrics and what is true to the human spirit. Applying metrics to an ideal is not easy: statistics are more easily applied to lower level aspirations and tangibles. The madness affecting schools is inherent in its focus on isolated metrics and attachment to processes and measurement.

Madness is not always violent or spectacular: sometimes it is indirect and subtle but just as volatile and disruptive. It can be the result of fiscal or political self-interest, the absurdity of political games, or the warp of inappropriate metaphors. The cliché that craziness is doing the wrong thing over and over again and expecting different results applies to school reform.

Educators have adopted scientific management approaches and logical step-by-step plans used in private sector manufacturing, service, and industry. Strategic planning, total quality management, metrical scorecards, power standards, and a spate of other processes are proposed. Private sector, profit-motive assumptions are seen as "the way" to run schools, approach change, and motivate people. These strategies emphasize cause-and-effect statistical accountability, along with hard-line consequences.

Everything that is important in schools is not measurable. How do you gauge the level of imagination, originality, or inspiration? What about passion and persistence? Can they be tabulated and charted?

The essence of what a school is and what it ought to be cannot be found in quantifiable data. Pursuing these approaches over the past decade has created a hollowness of effort, duplicity, and a deadened spirit. In fact, a case can be made that school reform proposals are failures if the data are scrutinized and closely examined.

This book is about the fog of reform and getting back the ideal of a place called school. The book defines a new metaphor and approach to change and examine the forces and ideals that can bring about the schools children need. Principles and values transform organizations, not mandates and fear. Recipes for making schools into caring places for children do not exist. Great schools must be created one by one. Numbers don't create change; people and passion do.

The irony is that the answer to school improvement rests more in the heart than in the head. Schools with a strong heart and soul dedicated to noble ideas far outweigh rational plans designed to scientifically manage organizations and cultures. Children and their learning are more important and complex than that.

Becoming educated is more than a collection of numbers. Learning is more complex than analytics. Significant relationships cannot be formed through technocratic processes. A place called school helps children to grow and mature—to find their passion and live a life of meaning and happiness. To do so we must lift the fog of reform and see clearly with new eyes.

Part I

The Fog

I

THE FOG OF REFORM

Every quantitative measurement we have shows we are winning this war.—Robert S. McNamara

Today the memory of the Vietnam conflict is fading. Time has passed, and new generations have no direct remembrance of that historical period or of the turmoil and frustration that bled into the politics and daily lives of citizens and communities. The war fractured society and became the dominant topic of the nightly news and commentary.

Looking back, the Vietnam War provided valuable lessons about management and leadership that can guide us in the future. Secretary of Defense Robert S. McNamara was the person most responsible—next to the president—for leading this conflict. McNamara was a "Whiz Kid," one of a group of ten statistical control experts who were known for their intelligence and coldly rational approaches to business. They promoted quantitative approaches and analysis to operations and accountability. To them, numbers equated to rational truth, which was supposed to translate into strategy and success.

According to John Byrne, "the Whiz Kids became architects of a new economic order that valued analysis over experience, numbers over intuition, and facts over emotion."[1] Renowned for their hubris and arrogance, they created a system of empirical data that basically taught managers to trust numbers more than people. Rational management based on metrics was the approach. The fallout was that out of numbers coupled with command and control procedures come answers.

McNamara believed that truth rested in numerical data. He brought cost-benefit analyses, ratios, data points, control systems, management information systems, and decision science to his work, whether as an army air force officer during World War II, president of Ford Motor Company, or secretary of defense during the Kennedy and Johnson administrations. He was obsessed with optimizing efficiency and improving effectiveness through quantitative measures and rational analysis.

McNamara and the Whiz Kids believed that value should be assigned to what can be quantified to create better accountability for decision making and outcomes. Technology and logic ruled. What was not easily quantifiable was overlooked; there was no way to measure intangibles because they were open to interpretation, bias, and emotion. The Whiz Kids believed in the infallibility of numbers because they thought that hard numbers eliminated bias or undocumented human judgment.

The Defense Department during this time focused on such metrics as "body counts" and "kill ratios." Statistics became the controlling measuring stick used to compare units' effectiveness. In a speech in 1962 concerning the Vietnam War, McNamara indicated that "every quantitative measurement we have shows we are winning this war."[2] How wrong he was. Only 2 percent of America's generals at that time thought that body count was a valid statistic; one general wrote that it was "totally worthless" and often a false and exaggerated statistic.[3] The single-minded emphasis on quantifiable analysis led to serious and grave errors.

As historians look in retrospect, there was bias in the data, some were of poor quality, some were misanalyzed or used misleadingly, and much failed to capture what they were meant to assess in the first place. In essence, people provided the data they thought the generals wanted. They provided data desirable to protect their positions out of concern for their own performance evaluations. They had to achieve the desired numbers. "Results were, it was suspected, sometimes faked, since certain other reporters were grading their own progress. When higher commanders rode lower ones for better statistical results, it was evident that they were going to get either the statistics or the results, and on fortunate occasions both."[4]

Statistics really didn't indicate how the war was going, and they missed entirely the intangible issues in the conflict. Wishful thinking or overly optimistic or pessimistic analysis actually missed the bigger and deeper picture of issues and outcomes.

The Pentagon and political leaders failed to take into account intangibles such as commitment, patriotism, hope, passion, courage, loyalty, responsibility, and others. But yet when we examine great achievements and accomplishments, issues like perseverance and heart are critical. In the Vietnam War, body counts were less important than commitment and loyalty to the cause.

McNamara's approach resulted in a misleading picture that was labeled "McNamara's Fallacy," also known as quantitative fantasy. Sociologist Daniel Yankelovich summarized McNamara's Fallacy in four steps:

- Measure what can be measured. This is fine as far as it goes.
- Disregard that which can't be measured or give it an arbitrary quantitative value. This is arbitrary and misleading.
- Presume that what can't be measured easily really isn't very important. This is blindness.
- Say that what can't be easily measured really doesn't exist. This is madness.[5]

So what does this have to do with school reform? The documentary about Vietnam entitled *The Fog of War* discusses McNamara's approach through interviews with him. The "fog" was created by the metrical approach to decision making, the lack of concern for intangibles, and the failure to question the basic assumptions behind the war to begin with—all relevant to current education reform approaches.

McNamara may have failed because he "was a hedgehog rather than a fox, an engineer rather than ecologist. The hedgehog knows one big thing, and for McNamara that was rational systems analysis. If he'd been a fox, he'd have brought additional perspectives to America's pressing problems. Like a dogged engineer, he believed that you could model and manipulate the inputs and outputs of any system. Unlike the ecologist, he didn't seem to appreciate the complexity of systems involving living things. If the variables explaining poverty or victory in guerrilla warfare were unwieldy or unmeasurable, he simply ignored them."[6]

When human beings are involved, metrics do not always reflect reality or predict behavior. Seeing the complexity in human endeavors is necessary because simplistic measurements do not provide a complete and valid picture. Motives and emotion cannot be calibrated through statistics. A leader's judgment, not simply quantitative analysis, is essential in dynamic, complex systems.

McNamara's obituary in the *Economist* stated, "He was haunted by the thought that amid all of the objective-setting and evaluating, the careful counting and cost-benefit analysis, stood ordinary human beings. They behaved unpredictably."[7] In essence, humans are well intentioned but do not always behave in formulaic or anticipated ways. We all have biases of judgment and do not always respond algorithmically—perspectives change and cognitive and emotional reactions do not follow prescriptions or expectations.

The same is true with school reform. A dense fog surrounding the reform movement exists for the same reasons. We have a penchant to believe numbers and think metrics accurately define reality. How can you argue with statistics? Hard numbers supposedly don't lie. That approach and attitude existed in both the Kennedy and Johnson administrations during the war.

Unless we realize that this fog exists in education, we will never get to a place called school that is appropriate and successful for children. What is manifest is not the issue. What is emerging—what is around the bend in the road—is what creates the future and havoc for data and plans. Chaos and irrationality exist and are a part of all open social systems. When we look back, we see serendipity and chance that plays in life.

The Whiz Kids taught us important lessons. First, we have to be aware of our limits to quantify key issues concerning school reform. Second, if we can quantify key issues, we should make sure that they give us real insight into the overall problem and not take us on an excursion through diverting weeds like the kill ratios, body count, percentages of roads secured.

In his 1995 memoir two decades after the war ended, McNamara feared that rational people could lead us to nuclear war and that rationality will not save us. He indicated that he failed to question basic assumptions that supported the war effort. The "domino theory" was a primary reason for becoming involved in that war, and few in the government challenged that theory or its premise. Ultimately, the belief in the domino theory undergirding all the quantifiable data was wrong. In addition, the accuracy of the metrics themselves was suspect regarding the success of the war effort.

We must challenge school reformers' assumptions and question what their definition of education is. We must challenge what approach is appropriate to ensure that our children and citizenry are well educated. Few raise these issues. Instead, we have fallen into the McNamara-like approach of centralized control and tactics emphasizing standardized test scores, inspections, teacher evaluations based on metrics, and ignoring the other data and intangibles that are critical in successful learning environments.

The dysfunctions and ethically questionable patterns in the Vietnam experience exist in education reform and the media. The continual and incessant testing of students and using questionable value-added and other approaches assumes that improvement occurs by consistently measuring it. All of this appears so scientific.

High-stakes measurements are not indicative of quality education. Like field commanders, individuals in schools provide the data that they think the centralized leaders desire so that they look good in the performance of their jobs and withhold data or information that paints a negative picture. The Atlanta test manipulation and other cheating scandals in the United States are evidence of the weakness of the Whiz Kid approach to management and leadership in education.

Quantifiable approaches fail to consider that students are not simple numbers and that they come to school with tangible and intangible cognitive, physical, and emotional issues that affect their performance. Home life, poverty, health, nutrition, drugs, and community or domestic violence affect their behavior. In reality, teaching is based on relationships with students, as well as teachers' passion and commitment.

McNamara and the Whiz Kids were perceived and caricatured as "smart but not wise"—leaders obsessed with narrow quantitative measures who lacked human understanding and perspective of the larger, complex picture. Some reformers show the same qualities: smart but not wise.

The lessons of McNamara are pertinent today in school reform. The numerical fetish in pursuit of big data and quantification can be misleading and not suitable for creating schools and classrooms that nourish children's curiosity, hearts, and souls. Wisdom is important, not only in management, but also as a goal of well-educated people.

As Charles Handy, the Irish author and philosopher specializing in organizational behavior management, stated in an interview entitled "The Future of Work in a Changing World":

> In the past, management studies have concentrated on analytic skills—analyzing the future, analyzing the market, analyzing the cost, analyzing the resources—and the idea was if the analysis was right, then plans could be put into action.
>
> Now a new set of softer skills are needed, skills to get people committed and excited. I like to talk about the "e" factors in organizations, "e" meaning all the words that start with "e," like excitement, effervescent, enthusiasm, energy. These new skills are far more difficult to teach in classrooms. You can talk about them and describe them in classrooms, but you can't really practice them in classrooms.[8]

Handy also advised that in school we should find out what each child's capacity is, build on it, and complement it. Real experience and wisdom matter.

We cannot let the "fog of reform" obscure our vision in getting back to a place called school, where children can grow, believe, and learn. Quantitative data can be important, but they are not a panacea for decisions, and they are not without serious limitations. Statistics can paint an inaccurate picture of conditions or progress in education. A rise in test scores does not always mean an increase in learning.

TYRANNY OF THE TANGIBLE

Public education has suffered from the tyranny of the tangible. The penchant to judge schools and teachers on the basis of test scores, graduation rates, suspension rates, or other metrics has run wild. In the debate about public schools, it basically boils down to "if you can't measure it, it doesn't matter." Schools appear to be successful if they get the numbers.

Schools worship on the altar of old-time scientific management and analytics. Data is the rage—big or otherwise. Data mapping. Data scanning. Data management. Data analysis. Data mining. Data-based decisions. We are immersed in numbers, algorithms, formulas, and metrics. In schools, students are reduced to numbers—test scores, absences, IQs, SATs, grades, and grade point averages.

What are lost in statistical analysis are the intangibles that are absolutely essential for educating and caring for children. In reality, schools are human, not technical, organizations. They are supposed to be principled and compassionate sanctuaries for children to grow and thrive. Human connection and common goals make up the essence of schools. Human relationships are fundamental.

Children are not products or miniature workers and certainly not "human capital." They are simply children who need nurturing and direction to develop in positive ways. We know that trouble and confusion are constants in life, and some children carry the heavy effects of socioeconomic factors beyond their control. Scientific management methods, however, offer feeble analysis or solutions for confronting the disequilibrium of life and the irrational environment in which some children live.

All parents want their children to go to a good school, another one of those abstract ideas that everyone supports but that is difficult to define. There is no statistic for it. No yardstick that measures its increase or decrease. Because some schools get better metrics does not necessarily make them "good" schools.

The intangibles related to goodness are not easily reduced to a scorecard or number. A "good" school is not a three on a five-point Likert scale between poor and excellent. Statistics cannot capture the aura of a "good" school or the intangible qualities that make teachers significant to students, just as numbers cannot capture the extent of love, compassion, or creativity.

Goodness involves the sensitivity to do what is "right" and fair in relationships and involves human decency, kindness, politeness, compassion, generosity, mercy, fairness, and respect. As a result of the goodness that comes from teachers, children are able to meet their promise and act in positive and constructive ways personally, socially, and politically. There is good will in the school toward others, and good habits of the mind and body are taught and reinforced. A moral dimension based on fundamental ethical values that require wisdom and judgment is evident and demands courage to do what is right and restraint to do no harm.

Goodness is connected to other great ideas—liberty, equality, and justice. Without those three, can people live happy lives and feel respected? Each of these is a part of life, and all should be a part of schools. We just need to recognize it and get back to a place called school. Goodness and all the descriptors for it are beyond simple metrics but are those things people feel and desire.

The tyranny of the tangible is obvious when schools and educators kowtow to the pressure of test scores or other metrics. The domino effect of assessing teachers on standardized test scores results in emphasizing test preparation, narrowing the curriculum to what's tested, pressuring children to succeed, and eliminating other activities that stimulate creativity and critical thinking—projects, exploring, questioning, or experimenting. Moving beyond superficial test scores to creative and critical thought takes time. In addition, children grow at different rates: sometimes in quick spurts and others in longer sequences that aren't on a consistent timetable or in linear fashion.

Being educated is much more than statistics: it concerns the intersection of the heart and mind with self-confidence, honor, and determination. A quote attributed to Einstein carries an important message for schools and all of us: "Not everything that can be counted counts, and not everything that counts can be counted."

As we mature we see the fallacy of metrical analyses in our lives. Are we our bank accounts? Are we our salary, blood pressure, net worth, IQ score, zip code, or SAT score? As we get older, we realize that all these data are not of much value in assessing a good life. Can a human being be reduced to a simplistic formula or can a life and its potential be summed up in a graph? Obviously, there are no simple metrics for leading a good life or for happiness.

Why do we reduce children and their education to test scores—proficiency, value added, conceptual, whatever? We take our most cherished and vulnerable people—our children—and reduce and assess them on simplistic and often erroneous statistics. Children are more than that. There are plenty of great people—creative people, courageous people, compassionate people, heroic people—who did not get the so-called numbers in school but made a difference in their family, community, or nation.

People are complex human beings whose imagination, virtue, determination, and other characteristics are beyond measurement. Technological data analysis cannot determine the value of people. Their "bigness" comes from their hearts, not from numbers, and their potential is nourished by teachers and mentors who believe in them and in their developing potential. Unique individuals progress through the nurturing of human interaction and relationships, not computers, data, or avatars.

Educational reformers should know that. If they don't, they should get their noses out of the metrics and sit and talk with eleven year olds so they can see what's really important in developing principled, intelligent, and caring individuals. Isn't that the goal to which we all aspire for our children?

Unless we focus on the moral imperative of educating children, we will fail them and possibly even slide into an ethical quagmire. The lessons of McNamara's Vietnam and other historical situations are testament to the fallacy of measuring progress simply by metrics. Instead of clarity, statistics can often provide an incomplete or inaccurate, foggy picture.

In actuality, the intangibles—principles, values, and ethics—that we desire in schools are the foundation for their integrity, credibility, and ultimately their effectiveness. Schools as sanctuaries for children provide high levels of care, compassion, and patience as students work their way to maturity. Actually, helping and encouraging children to find meaning and fulfillment is an act of love—not a technical quantitative exercise.

ESSENTIAL IDEAS TO REMEMBER

- McNamara's Fallacy is at work in school reform.
- Data analysis is not infallible and does not present an accurate picture of circumstances.
- A fog can be created by overreliance on statistical analysis based on faulty assumptions that obscure clear thinking and incalculable forces.
- There are limits to quantifying student progress and growth because learning is more complex than a single statistic like a test score.

- Questioning assumptions undergirding any major effort, including reforms, is necessary to avoid misdirected efforts and inappropriate data.
- There are intangibles in any human enterprise, which can be the determining factors in success or failure.
- Children are not conglomerations of metrics that can be easily measured.

NOTES

1. John A. Byrne, *The Whiz Kids* (New York: Currency Doubleday 1993), 515.
2. Douglas Kinnard, *The War Managers* (Annapolis, MD: Naval Institute Press, 1979), 73.
3. Kenneth Cukier and Vicktor Mayer-Schonberger, "The Dictatorship of Data," *MIT Technology Review*, May 31, 2013, 1.
4. Kinnard, 71.
5. Daniel Yankelovich, "Corporate Priorities: A Continuing Study of the New Demands in Business," 1972, http://schoollibrary.org/articles/McNamara_fallacy.
6. Thomas H. Davenport, "Robert McNamara's Good Brain—and Bad Judgment," *Harvard Business Review*, July 7, 2009, https://hbr.org/2009/07/robert-s-mcnamaras-good-brain/.
7. *Economist*, obituary, "Robert McNamara, Systems Analyst and Defense Secretary, Died on July 6th, Aged 93," July 9, 2009.
8. Charles Handy, "The Future of Work in a Changing World," *Aurora* (fall 1991), http://aurora.icaap.org/index.php/aurora/article/view/52/65.

2

FOG AND ETHICAL PITFALLS

> Like a man traveling in foggy weather, those at some distance before him on the road he sees wrapped up in the fog, as well as those behind him, and also the people in the fields on each side, but near him all appears clear, although in truth he is as much in the fog as any of them.—Benjamin Franklin

Historically, public schools were not seen as part of the "marketplace." They were part of the community, a resource, a meeting place, a source of local pride: it was a place called school, filled with hope, cooperation, and destiny. It had all the intangible and noble attributes that a market-driven monolith like Wal-Mart or other large corporations wish they had. Public schools were seen as a responsible, trustworthy, positive common good.

Significant differences exist between institutions vital to our society and competitive, profit-oriented, market-driven corporate entities. Do people really think corporations are illustrative of goodness and the common good? In fact, a 2015 Gallup poll indicated that only 21 percent of the public had confidence in big business, just a notch above its confidence in Congress.[1]

Two infamous streets in New York City—Wall Street and Madison Avenue—have had tremendous impact on the United States and the world. The interesting thing is that the fundamental values of both concern self-interest through marketing and profits. A cynic might say that the quote attributed to P. T. Barnum, "there's a sucker born every minute," describes the operating philosophy behind both, particularly Madison Avenue.

With Madison Avenue come slogans. Remember "plop plop, fizz fizz, oh what a relief it is," "think different," "like a good neighbor," or "sometimes you feel like a nut, sometimes you don't"? And who can forget, "where's the beef?"? We all know the impact of Madison Avenue in politics. Catchphrases. Poll-tested language. Code words. Obfuscation. Misinterpretations. Brand and image are all important.

Education today is not immune to marketing tactics using such innocuous slogans and catchphrases, for example, "students first," "no child left behind," "blended instruction," "race to the top," "measurable results," "knowledge is power," "personalized education," "value added," or "21st-century skills." What do they all mean, really? Along with slogans come false claims, misinterpretation of data, oversimplification of issues, and, certainly, distortion and falsehoods.

Special interest dominates marketing and advertising. With education, however, special interest should not apply. Children's learning and welfare should be based on values and the common good, not special interest.

Well, Madison Avenue, along with its strategies, culture, and politics, has infiltrated public education. What used to be considered the staid and boring area of K–12 education is now in the same category as any other market. *Forbes* magazine predicted back in 1998 that education would emerge as one of the leading investment sectors over the next 20 years.

Today, educational celebrities have sprung up in the educational reform movement. Michelle Rhee became, to some, the face of educational reform, even though her record was questionable. Certainly Bill Gates has turned his fortune in technology into a celebrity influence on what your child should experience and learn in school, of course, with heavy utilization of technology and testing. So-called American icons like Oprah Winfrey gave millions to charter schools across the country. Campbell Brown, former news anchor on CNN, champions the elimination of teacher tenure, as does Whoopi Goldberg. Both see teachers and unions as the problem, and have connections for instant media exposure.

Media sound bites escalate rather than generate serious dialogue about what education is, what accountability means, or the impact of poverty and social issues on children's ability to succeed. Maybe "where's the beef?" is the slogan we should ask of reformers, media, special interests, and politicians.

The "beef" may not be there. In a study on education and the media, Malin and Lubienski found that "permanent interest groups are promoting reform agendas and striving to influence policymakers and public opinion using individuals who have substantial media skills but little or no expertise and education research."[2] The researchers indicated that individuals with less expertise but with media skills have greater success in "media penetration."

According to Media Matters, in 2014 only 9 percent of television guests discussing education on evening cable news were educators.[3] On CNN, Fox News, and MSNBC, the percentages of educators discussing education were 4 percent, 5 percent, and 14 percent, respectively. The vast majority of guests on those media outlets were individuals with little or no experience or expertise in education. Many have degrees in government or law or ties to foundations, think tanks, or corporations with self-interest in education. Wealth and celebrity do not signify expertise and commitment.

With corporate or celebrity sponsored reforms come a focus on market, competition, and choice. Education has become a booming market for business. The so-called market is supposed to improve education because of choice. Privatize education and the problems disappear because the market will reward excellence and penalize failure.

In 1955 economist Milton Friedman argued that the free market was the only way to reform schools. The profit motive would produce an array of schools and choice. The result is the growth of an "education-industrial complex." The education-industrial complex is the fusion of corporations and government with a broad array of education industries. And, of course, companies pitch mandates to politicians in Washington, DC, and in state capitals so that their materials, tests, and technology can produce profit.

This complex pushes for programs and technology and then sells programs, products, and services to provide for them. "At the heart of the education-industrial complex is the public purse held by federal, state, and local school district governments. Collected from tax revenues, the public purse tempts education entrepreneurs interested in profiting from taxpayers' money. One key to opening the public largess to for-profit companies [is] educational policies that favor for-profit schools, colleges, educational management organizations, the purchase of school equipment, books, tests, software, and the use of supplementary education services such as tutoring."[4]

In Minnesota, free-market approaches were tried for two decades through charters, open enrollments, and school choice with no marked improvements in graduation rates or achievement. However, the study found that market drive caused increases in public relations efforts and "teaching to the test." The Minnesota Policy Institute concluded that the "market place metaphor does not apply to education" and that its application can "corrupt some policies that have legitimate educational purposes and divert attention to other policies—like voucher programs—that will not succeed."[5]

Testing companies like Pearson and publishers that produce curriculum materials around mandated tests and programs are a growing and profitable part of the national economy. These companies have been active in national and state policy discussions with the aim of profits. Decisions about education influence the bottom-line profits and losses of large corporations like Pearson.

Would Pearson do what's best for children if its bottom line is threatened? A company like Rocketship uses technology in a so-called blended computer-based approach, reducing the number of teachers and replacing them with aides. Technology and aides and fewer teachers may save money for the corporation, but is it the best for children and their learning?

Obviously, if privatization occurs on a large scale, education companies stand to profit from public money. As the education-industrial complex games policy decisions through lobbyists and other means, the direction of education will be out of the direct control of school boards and citizens. Profits are the first priority of the educational-industrial complex, not the education of children.

PRIVATIZATION

Advocates perceive privatization as the answer to better schools and education in the form of vouchers, tuition tax credits, education management organizations (EMOs), private contractors, charter management organizations, and virtual schools.

Efforts to privatize education lead to an emphasis on "consumer goods," not the common good: "Democracy is about making wise collective choices, not individual consumer choices. Democracy and education and education and democracy are not quaint legacies from a distant and happier time. They had never been more essential to wise self-rule than they are today."[6]

Public schools were created to impart the values of our nation and to educate children so that they can contribute and participate in our society politically, socially, and economically. They were created for the common good, not for profit.

Businesses, on the other hand, are created for providing a service or product with the express purpose of making profit. Money is to be made. But profit can distort decision making. Profits can come before pupils. In this case the old adage "the buyer beware" may be the principle that parents will need to embrace if privatization takes hold.

Parents and others have a place to be heard if they are dissatisfied with public education. If they are disgruntled with Pearson's test materials, where can they go? If the for-profit Rocketship schools are not meeting their responsibilities, where do parents go? Will Bill Gates respond to parents who disagree with the teacher evaluation schemes that he's been promoting? Once public policy is manipulated into mandates or legislation for the gain of special or personal interests, citizens lose control, and changing them is not easy.

The upshot of corporate influences, of course, systematically reduces democratic control of schools. Are corporations going to be more responsive to your needs than your local school board? As a citizen, are you really going to have any input into the policies and procedures—not to mention the goals of the curriculum—if a corporation runs a school, particularly if profit or special interests are involved? Is transparency of finances and policy lost when schools are privatized?

Foundations like the Melinda and Bill Gates Foundation, the GE Foundation, and the Walton Family Foundation encouraged the blossoming of for-profit education companies like Apex Learning, Pearson, Charter Schools USA, VSCHOOLZ, News Corp., Microsoft, Intel, and K12 Inc.[7] In addition, think tanks on both sides of the political ledger are involved: American Enterprise Institute, the Center for American

Progress, and the Center on Reinventing Public Education, among others.

The privatization movement actually undermines a fundamental and traditional value of public education as a foundation for a better life individually and collectively through community commitment and support. Eliminating public schools removes oversight, leaving education to the whim of entrepreneurs and financiers. This certainly will jeopardize what the goals of education should be.

Are schools simply places to control and train future compliant workers and consumers? Or are they places that produce individuals who are skeptical, critical, independent thinkers willing to challenge and act in the public interest, not corporate or individual self-interest?

A prime example is Pearson, which is a major corporation producing many of the standardized tests that children take across the nation. The Gates Foundation and the Pearson Corporation, a British company, have joined in the development of the Common Core standards. Pearson, of course, stands to profit from Common Core assessments. Testing is obviously a big portion of that approach, which has propelled the focusing of instruction on the adopted standards.

Pearson's operating 2012 profit in the educational market was $1.4 billion. In 2015, Pearson determined that it was going to focus solely on the international education market rather than any other interest. It is possible for American children in grades K–12 to take Pearson designed tests, to use Pearson-designed curricula materials, and to be taught by teachers certified by a Pearson test.[8]

All that we have to do is think about American and international corporations and their concern for American citizens. The record on Wall Street and in the automobile, pharmaceutical, food, tobacco, and other industries demonstrates that the corporate profits, not people, come first. That's totally antithetical to the mission of public education in our country. Public schools were designed to provide all children, regardless of background, an opportunity to become educated and to have the opportunity to fully participate in our democracy.

As citizens, we should be concerned that a historic foundation of our democracy—public education—is in jeopardy and could become a market for corporations that emphasize profits rather than the education of all children. Evidence indicates that these approaches and charter schools do not educate a cross section of the population.

Charter schools operated by EMOs have become the "wonder drug" of educational reform. While the media continually expound on the failure of public education, charter schools are perceived as a solution, even though research demonstrates otherwise. According to Stanford University's Center for Research on Education Outcomes Study, "there are still urban communities in which the majority of the charter schools have smaller learning gains compared to their traditional school counterparts."[9]

In another study on charter schools, Stanford University's Center for Research found:

- Of the 2,403 charter schools reflected on the curve, 46 percent of charter schools have math gains that are statistically indistinguishable from the average growth among their traditional public school (TPS) comparisons.
- Charters whose math growth exceeded their TPS equivalent growth by a significant amount account for 17 percent of the total.

The remaining group, 37 percent of charter schools, posted math gains that were significantly below what their students would have achieved if they enrolled in local traditional public schools instead.[10]

With schools, operations and decisions must be credible and ethical. In the market, competition rules, and data and information can be biased and skewed to promote and sell programs. Do you really believe marketing and advertising is objective and accurate? Ethical pitfalls can distort the picture.

DECISIONS AND ETHICAL PITFALLS

In this contemporary milieu of reform, reformers push proposals and their wares and build alliances with foundations and politicians in order to reach their goals.

But there are problems. Real problems.

A major issue is: How can you be assured that the suggested reform, policy, and educational decisions are appropriate and right? Are they effective? Are they ethical?

Today's schools focus on tangibles that translate into ratios, scores, and ratings, which can result in simplistic and one-dimensional judgments about "quality." The emphasis on metrics alone can result in decisions that are ethically questionable, as proven by other historic events.

> We are more susceptible than we think to the dictatorship of data—that is, to letting the data govern us in ways that may do as much harm as good. The threat is that we will let ourselves be mindlessly bound by the output of our analysis even when we have reasonable grounds for suspecting that something is amiss. Education seems on the skids? Push standardized tests to measure performance and penalize teachers or schools.[11]

Educational triage is a prime example. To improve schools' performance on high stakes tests, priority and emphasis is placed on helping those students who are *close* to achieving proficiency—for example, students who need to correctly answer two to four more questions—at the expense of spending more time with students who are further from demonstrating competence and moving the metrical needle. In other situations, students who do not fit the mold are not enrolled in the school or are "counseled out," thereby creating a more select student group that is more likely to achieve higher on tests.

Stressing high-stakes testing and other metrical drives can turn classrooms into high-pressure, competitive environments creating "haves and have-nots." Time and the clock work on teachers and students, resulting in a harried and unhealthy climate. Ethical pitfalls occur when pressure is placed to get the desired numbers.

One pitfall is self-protection. Individuals, driven by the need for approval and winning support, are concerned primarily with themselves—their advancement, acceptance, or ego. Looking good is the goal. They "pass the buck," tell others what they want to hear, or "slick over" information by putting it into the best or most positive light to win favor.

Self-righteousness is another trap. There's a difference between passion and self-righteousness. Certainly, enthusiasm is a positive force. But zealots who are convinced of the rightness of their cause will go to almost any means to push it. Listening drops by the wayside and arguing boils up. Remember Machiavelli's dictum—the means justifies the ends rings true here because people are convinced that the nobility of their cause justifies questionable methods. Honor, truth, integrity, and principle become victims as people, procedures, and data are abused.

Self-deception can be a by-product of individuals accommodating and compromising. This is inevitable in decision making, but it is the ethical nature of the compromise that is of concern. People get in trouble because they go along with the leaders or group even if their principles are compromised. For example, individuals may ditch ethical principles to push the boss's questionable agenda, cause, or program. In these situations, the "best face" is put on the circumstances, and people excuse these indiscretions in the name of progress and the cynical realities of the world.

Self-protection, self-righteousness, and self-deception are powerful hidden influences on decisions and actions. Reform or work groups can trigger them because of the very dynamics of corporate, public, or political work. All you have to do is watch people's behavior in groups to see the potential problems.

Group shift is another ethical problem facing causes and groups, which occurs when individuals do not question fundamental assumptions or challenge the substance of collective decisions. McNamara warned of this. Individuals go along because they fear for their own interests if they challenge assumptions, go against the grain, and question colleagues or current initiatives. Going along with the group can be convenient, but it can be hazardous personally and collectively. Standing alone as the lone wolf howling in the wilderness takes courage.

Professionals have a calling that should temper any ethical trap through standards of conduct, values, and ethics. Professionals cannot duck responsibility and maintain credibility and commitment to their ethics. There are ethical standards against which behavior, decisions, and procedures are assessed. Professionals have an obligation to:

- Be accountable for their actions and for the individual actions they initiate at the direction of others. Following orders does not lessen individual responsibility.
- Understand that inaction, like overt conduct, can result in unethical behavior. To stand and do nothing is not always a benign act. Inaction is a decision that can be harmful.

- Accept responsibility for their subordinates, peers, or others if they encourage them to behave unethically.

Individuals must counter "group think" or going along with the crowd if ethical standards are compromised. Ethics are powerful, invisible structures that are self-monitoring, if they are clear and understood.

Political or social movements carry ethical responsibilities for individual and collective decisions and behavior. Professionals stand up, individually or collectively, if ethical breaches occur. We need to think about that in reform efforts and all decisions in public schools.

Collecting, reporting, and acting on data must be ethically and procedurally correct. We need to challenge studies and so-called research and question their validity and reliability. Sometimes false conclusions are drawn from research data.

ICE CREAM AND MURDER

What do ice cream and murder have to do with school reform? It's hard to believe, but there appears to be a correlation between homicides and ice cream sales. When ice cream sales increase, the homicide rate increases. Data and statistics demonstrate that connection.

Can we conclude that there is a direct connection between ice cream sales and murder? By looking at simple statistics and numbers, one can deduce that as people consume more ice cream, murder is the result. If that's the case, maybe we should stop selling ice cream.

Actually, the relationship between ice cream and murder is a coincidence. There is evidence to suggest that murder rates increase when the seasonal temperature rises. Same with ice cream sales. When the weather warms, people get together, there is much more social interaction, both positive and negative. In addition, public drinking and drug use increases. Hence, ice cream may not be a cause of an uptick in the murder rate. At play are other things that influence those statistics.

Although the data are statistically correct, the conclusion is absolutely wrong. This is an example of disestimation, only one hazard of research studies and data. Besides drawing false conclusions, there are

FOG AND ETHICAL PITFALLS

other flawed interpretations as well as unethical manipulation of statistics and research.

We are enamored with metrics and data. Madison Avenue marketers are specialists in providing convincing figures about products and businesses. Politicians use opinion polls to mold their words. And, of course, the quality of a school or your child's ability is reduced to simplistic statistics.

This is all nice and neat: everything in life is reduced down to numbers that seem so scientific, rational, and objective. We think numerical data are free of bias and prejudice. The inarguable truth! Statistics seemingly communicate objectivity and certainty. But do they—really?

Data collection and interpretation must undergo ethical checks because data can be deceiving. After all, data are supposed to be turned into information, which is then used to make judgments and decisions. Just because information and conclusions are wrapped in numbers does not make them any truer than written stories or arguments. Data can be used to lie, present false conclusions, or skew arguments to a particular point of view.

Proofiness: The Dark Arts of Mathematical Deception describes ways that data can be manipulated unethically:

- Disestimation: We fall prey to believing that numbers and statistics are an absolute truth, and we ascribe too much meaning to them, giving them more significance than they deserve. We present them as the total truth and ignore any uncertainties that surround them and their collection. Simplistic numbers are not always accurate or truthful in evaluating the complexities of life or people. Remember, ice cream and murder!
- Cherry picking: Cherry picking is a deception based on selecting data that support your position or argument while underplaying or ignoring data that oppose it. Accentuate the positive—ignore the negative. In essence, you don't give the whole picture or tell the whole truth. Selective use of data is prevalent in politics and, unfortunately, in schools, too (for example, by using the only positive test score when the remaining scores are mediocre).
- Potemkin numbers: These numbers look like data and are presented like accurate data, but they are built on a facade. Potemkin numbers are phony statistics based on erroneous or nonexistent

calculations. They are manufactured metrics. The presenter of the Potemkin numbers makes them up, sometimes through a scientific-looking nonsensical measurement. Schemers use this strategy because they know our penchant for believing in numerical data, even if fabricated.

- Comparing apples and oranges: Test scores are frequently used for comparing student achievement. In comparing the performance of two groups, both must have the same characteristics. The ethical problem is comparing the performance of two distinct groups and drawing conclusions as if the groups were similar in characteristics. That's why statistics between charter schools and public schools are difficult to sort out, for example, comparing a cohort group of students who experienced an entire program to a random sample of students who may not have experienced the entire program. We are comparing oranges to grapefruits—they are all citrus, but quite different because one is a specialized group and the other is random cross section. In another example, some charter schools do not accept new students after fourth grade. The specialized cohort group is then compared on standardized tests to public schools that are required to take all students who come to their doors before or after fourth grade and may not have experienced the total program.
- Charts and graphs: Data are frequently presented in chart or graph form. There may be nothing inherently inaccurate about the data; however, accurate data presented in a graph and chart can be deceptive if the left axis numerical scale is manipulated to show larger gains or smaller losses. Differences look larger or smaller based on the left axis number spread.[12]

Numbers are not cold, hard facts. They can be deceptive through unethical comparisons, presentation, or falsehoods. We must guard against being deceived through the techniques above that result in lies, fabrications, or half-truths. People have motives, and those motives can distort the collection, interpretation, and presentation of data.

Intangibles like creativity, passion, and commitment cannot be reduced to a simplistic metric. Neither can commitment, loyalty, justice, beauty, liberty, or any other principle or value.

ESSENTIAL IDEAS TO REMEMBER

- The corporate privatization efforts in education have consequences for children and the future of our society and government.
- Special interests and the profit motive in education can jeopardize the common good and the goals and outcomes of education in the United States.
- Data and statistics must be reported correctly and ethically if they are to be used in decision making about children's education.
- Ethical pitfalls endanger the credibility and integrity of organizations and individuals.

NOTES

1. Gallup poll, http://www.gallup.com/poll/1597/confidence-institutions.aspx.

2. Joel R. Malin and Christopher Lubienski, "Educational Expertise, Advocacy, and Media Influence," *Education Policy Analysis Archive*, 23, no. 6, January 26, 2015.

3. *Media Matters*, "New Study Highlights Lack of Education Experts in Point and Online Media," February 23, 2015, http://mediamatters.org/blog/2015/02/23/new-study-highlights-lack-of-education-experts/202638.

4. Anthony G. Picciano, *The Great American Education Industrial Complex* (New York: Routledge, 2013), 168.

5. Michael Diedrich, "False Choices: The Economic Argument against Market Driven Education Reform," *Minnesota Policy Institute*, January 20, 2012, 30.

6. Sarah Mondale and Sara B. Patton, *School: The Story of American Education* (Boston: Beacon Press, 2001), 8.

7. *Washington Post*, "Jeb Bush's Education Foundation Releases Donor List a Day after His Tax Returns," July 1, 2015, www.washingtonpost.com/blogs/post-politics/wp/2015/07/01/jeb-bushs-education-foundation-releases-donor-list-a-day-after-his-tax-returns/.

8. Valerie Strauss, "Pearson Selling Some Investments to Be '100' Percent Focused on Education," *Washington Post*, July 26, 2015.

9. Stanford University, "Center for Research on Education Outcomes Study," 2015, http://urbancharters.stanford.edu/news.php, 2015.

10. Stanford University, "Multiple Choice: Charter School Performance in 16 States," Center for Research on Education Outcomes (CREDO), 2009,

http://credo.stanford.edu/reports/MULTIPLE_CHOICE_EXECUTIVE%20SUMMARY.pdf.

11. Kenneth Cukier and Vicktor Mayer-Schonberger, "The Dictatorship of Data," *MIT Technology Review*, May 31, 2013, 41.

12. Charles Seife, *Proofiness: The Dark Arts of Mathematical Deception* (New York: Viking, 2010).

3

ASSUMPTIONS, EVALUATION, AND CARROTS AND STICKS

> You can use all the quantitative data you can get, but you still have to distrust it and use your own intelligence and judgment.—Alvin Toffler

Reformers try to change how we perceive, think, and operate. Of course, they believe that they have the answers. Their view and perspective is outward, not inward. They think they are right, and in some cases become dogmatic and "true believers" in their cause. In a sense, they can become hedgehogs.

Challenging is the preferred tactic. Self-reflection is not in the cards. Sometimes, as time passes and they look back, reformers can see what they missed, didn't realize, or failed to understand. Retrospect clarifies thought.

Although it's healthy for the establishment to reflect, it's also desirable for reformers to do so. Reformers should examine their assumptions and reform their thinking. Robert McNamara, after years passed, said not doing so was strategically disastrous even with refined statistical analysis at his beck and call. Assumptions about the role and state of public education must be considered and appraised. Outcomes—both measurable and intangible—are involved.

After more than 25 years of national education reform, what has been the result? No Child Left Behind or Race to the Top all followed similar themes: high stakes testing, data-based metrics, carrots and sticks, disparagement of teachers and unions, and a romance with school choice.

Human development is not a race or a test. We must move beyond vacuous political slogans like Race to the Top. What race? What top? The result has been a flood of regulation initiatives that come and go. Maybe it's time to reform the reforms.

Exploring assumptions and revisiting some fundamental questions about reform can provide clarity, move us beyond politics and platitudes, and curtail damage from unanticipated consequences and closed thinking. Questioning basic assumptions is essential when the stakes are high in educating children.

- What is the basic assumption of reform concerning what constitutes an educated citizen?

    - What is an educated person?
    - Is there a difference between education and schooling?
    - Is passing a standardized test the marker of an educated person?
    - Is the goal of education about getting a college degree or job, or is there a larger purpose?
    - Are intangibles more important than tangibles when human effort is involved?
    - Where do character, commitment, creativity, ethics, and wisdom fit into an education?
    - Do children learn in "adequate yearly progress" segments?
    - Are the goals of education of reformers in line with the goal of producing skeptical and critical thinking individuals with a strong sense of our nation's values?

- What is the assumption behind the move to increase federal control of education?

    - Will centralized federal control of public education result in quality schools?
    - Do regulations from Washington produce innovative and dynamic schools?

- Do federal regulations create trickle-down taxation and red tape that puts a financial burden on states and local school boards?
- Should the nexus of control of education rest in Washington or the private sector?
- Do mandates spur creativity?

- What is the assumption behind privatization of U.S. education?

    - Will the profit motive produce greater emphasis on the needs of children?
    - Do parents want an education directed from corporations, special interests, or foundations?
    - Is it healthy for our democracy for public tax dollars to go to privatized organizations that lack political and financial transparency?
    - Are schools really businesses, and are children and parents really customers?
    - Are schools unique and different from profit-making or competitive organizations?
    - Is choice the panacea that improves student achievement?
    - Will privatization of schools really educate all children?
    - In light of research, are reform strategies like charter, voucher, and for-profit schools really successful?
    - Will a privatized system protect our democratic values and work for the common good?

- What are the assumptions about assessing education and teachers?

    - Has teaching to standardized tests narrowed the curriculum and restricted the achievement of more complex educational goals?
    - Is it ethical to evaluate teachers on test scores without defining the statistical limitations of the instruments?
    - Do multiple-choice tests taken by thirteen year olds really count for much in the long run?
    - Can teachers' effectiveness be quantified and reduced to multiple-choice tests?

- How do you evaluate teachers who do not teach the content tested?
- Are "value-added" approaches valid and reliable?
- Is the reliability of value-added instruments sufficient to be used for making valid decisions based on them?
- Is the role of a teacher no more than that of a computer avatar guiding instructional content?
- What do teachers control, and what are the "uncontrollables" that can overwhelm the instructional process?
- What is the responsibility of students and parents in learning and achievement?
- Do carrot-and-stick approaches motivate teachers to improve their performances and the schools?
- What are the dysfunctions of carrots and sticks and being married to bottom-line metrics?
- Is there a difference between motivation and movement?
- Are top-down inspections systems detrimental to creativity and innovation?

Sometimes the answers to these assumptions lie in the metaphors used to describe schools and their outcomes. Businesses or schools? Customers or students? Training or education? Compliance or creativity? Victims or players?

The reform movement has gotten a pass on some of these questions. Platitudes are not policy. Politics is not science. Special interests are not objective. Reform does not automatically mean improvement. Reviewing fundamental questions may cause us to stop and reflect and not engage in political and misdirected solutions.

Important questions. Important stakes. They produce important conversation and dialogue and raise questions about basic assumptions.

TEACHER EVALUATION

Imagine going to a physician and the doctor indicates that you have to change your lifestyle because your "numbers," based on a variety of tests, are not good. He prescribes a different diet, some medication, and a lifestyle change emphasizing physical activity and eliminating self-destructive behavior. He also wants to see you in three weeks to check on your progress.

You leave the office and fall into your usual behavior of eating the wrong foods and not exercising; in addition, you miss the next two appointments. When you do go back to the physician's office, your test numbers have not improved and in fact have gotten worse.

You made little or no effort to comply with the physician's instructions and, in effect, jeopardized your health. There is no "value-added" improvement. Whose fault is this? Should the physician lose his or her job? Was he or she ineffective and incompetent?

In many schools across the country, the fault rests with the teacher. If students and parents do not follow through on assignments, deadlines, attendance, or commitment, it becomes the teacher's fault. Students and parents are off the hook. Do students and parents have responsibilities for educational outcomes? Is that realistic?

At a time when we all want high quality education, politicians and bureaucrats are chasing simplistic and untested answers to improve teaching and learning. States "are racing ahead based on promises made to Washington or local political imperatives that prioritize an unwavering commitment to unproven approaches,"[1] says Grover J. Whitehurst, a senior fellow at the Brookings Institution. These approaches can have negative impacts on students and teachers.

On the surface, it seems simple. Test children to see if teachers are effective. But there are questions surrounding this initiative.

- Are the tests valid and reliable measures of student achievement?
- When analyzing the data, whose scores are included? Are students who were not in the class for the entire process included? What about special education students?
- Are the comparisons of achievement ethical, or do they compare a select group (like a cohort) to a random sample of the total population?
- What about transients? Some teachers face a continually changing student class load. Are teachers responsible for the achievement levels of students who did not participate in the entire process or program?

- What about teachers whose areas are not specifically tested—fine arts, physical education, foreign language, or social studies? How will they be assessed?
- Does the culture and climate of the entire school affect the classroom, instruction, and achievement?
- Is the research on value-added instruments reliable, producing consistent results over time?
- Are principals and superintendents culpable for the lack of student achievement based on test metrics?
- Is teaching simply following a recipe? Teaching is not just "doing" and implementing. Teaching is not simply implementing a recipe. It is not just "doing" and implementing. Teaching is more than that. It has to do with teachers and students "being" together in a creative and stimulating process.
- What about the attendance record of students? If a student attends school 62 percent of the time, can a teacher be held responsible for his or her academic performance?

Simplistic reliance on tests coupled with complicated rubrics can have devastating impacts. Who would want to work in a profession where you are held accountable for factors not within your control? Are creative and innovative people going to enter a profession that is perceived to be a technocratic activity rather than a professional obligation? Shouldn't accountability be a pillar of high ethics and well-researched design?

With all the curiosities occurring in school reform, teachers are in a different position. If you are a teacher, would you work in an impoverished community with kids who are poor, who have more learning needs, and who live in neighborhoods with serious problems and high crime rates? Or would you go to an upper-middle-class suburb where positive test performance is less of an issue? Precarious reforms can have unanticipated consequences.

Going back to the physician example, would you be perceived as more capable if you worked in a general hospital, as opposed to one that specializes in severe and critical illnesses? If you worked with severely ill patients or those with complex medical issues rather than those with routine medical problems, does the recovery rate accurately measure your performance?

Do we want smart, creative, and engaging teachers—as long as they paint by the numbers? Does that make sense to you? Or is there another way?

THE DARK SIDE OF REFORM

The merry-go-round of change during the past 40 years has made something that is complex by its very nature into a complicated and strangled enterprise. Change agents have pushed a cascade of reforms and fads that were supposed to be the keys to transformation, yet we've watched them come and go, leaving only jargon and cynicism. In many cases the reforms were failures.

Larry Cuban stated, "evaluating teachers on the basis of test scores, ending tenure and seniority, calling principals CEOs, and children learning to code will be like tissue-paper reforms of the past that have been crumpled up and tossed away."[2]

The result of this mind-set is more regulation, mandates, and red tape that demoralizes teachers and administrators. In actuality, educational systems comprise a web of relationships that do not always respond to the wishes of power brokers or machine-like tweaks and data-based lubrication.

Systems depend on people for change. If the system does not have certain qualities, it is destined for stagnation and rigor mortis. In addition to questioning assumptions, the keys to system resilience and growth include exploring and discussing ideas, maintaining the stability of organizational climate and culture, and creating the freedom to professionally experiment. Fear of failure drives out ideas and destroys creativity, sapping emotional and intuitive resources. When faced with challenges and changing contexts, people must be able to explore new possibilities and have the latitude to innovate.

Imposed mandates and regulations stifle and kill imagination and energy. Wrongheaded policies result in organizational distraction, often yielding unexpected and unhealthy results. Professionals do not follow meaningless and ethically questionable commands and initiatives. Some so-called reforms today create competition and distance between people, not collaboration, energy, and innovation. Meaning and values, not fear or money, motivate people to cooperate and perform at their highest levels.

The bottom line is simple. Bureaucratic demands and directives make education more complicated, resulting in less creative and imaginative education for children. False metrics and carrots and sticks requiring blind compliance create fear and drive out talent.

As teacher and principal autonomy are narrowed, discretion and freedom to imagine and problem solve are restricted or discouraged. Overregulation breeds moribund institutions focused on mandates rather than mission. Creative problem solving and risk taking become extinct as individuals toe the mark to avoid punishment or to obtain security. Intelligent and imaginative people are not attracted to a "paint-by-the-numbers" profession and a "get the numbers" mentality with punishing consequences for falling short.

The education-industrial complex is the recipient of sales and profit from legislated reforms. In an attempt to grapple with reform, some schools have sold their souls to the federal government's carrot-and-stick policies and programs in order to get the carrot—money. The sale has also been to the private sector and business leaders who extol hardheaded, bottom-line approaches to running organizations while foraging profit from public monies.

THE DARKNESS OF CARROTS AND STICKS

Daniel Pink, in his book *Drive: The Surprising Truth about What Motivates Us*, overturns the fallacy of carrot-and-stick approaches to human motivation. A big gulf exists between what science knows about motivation and what businesses and organizations do. Action due to force and anxiety is far different from motivation. People are *moved*, not motivated, by fear.

Pink states "carrots and sticks can achieve precisely the opposite of their intended aims. Mechanisms designed to increase motivation can dampen it. Tactics aimed at boosting creativity can reduce it. Programs to promote good deeds can make them disappear. Meanwhile, instead of restraining negative behavior, rewards and punishments often set it loose—and give rise to cheating, addiction, and dangerously myopic thinking."[3]

Prodding people with money is a bankrupt approach that establishes a culture of rewards based on compliance—following orders. Individuals get locked in a defined mind-set and a standard way of accomplishing work to get the reward. Carrots and sticks result in short-term thinking. Pink asserts "when institutions—families, schools, businesses, and athletic teams, for example—focus on the short term and opt for controlling people's behavior, they do considerable long-term damage." People forfeit some of their autonomy, lose control of their efforts, and limit the scope and depth of their thinking. Negative behavior is promoted resulting in deception, shortcuts, and unethical conduct in order to get the carrot.

The dysfunctional residue left by reforms like carrots and sticks is evident in some urban and suburban school districts across the country where test results and other data are "cooked" to produce the appearance of high performance. The so-called Texas education "miracle" used misleading dropout rates to bolster its claims. In Washington, DC, a highly touted high school turnaround was a deception. Pressure to get the numbers can lead to breaches of professional ethics.

The myth of the "take-no-prisoners," micromanaging leader charging through schools, using derision and fear may make celebrity icons, but it does nothing for creating a sustainable culture that nourishes people's desire to reach important goals. They ignore the power of intrinsic motivation as found in Frederick Herzberg's landmark motivation hygiene study. In fact, these ham-handed administrators destroy potential and motivation and confuse short-term action based on fear with motivation.

CONTEXT DOES MATTER

Some school reformers erroneously cite teachers as the most important factor in a child's education. The research really states that teachers are the most important *school-related* factor in a child's education.

That distinction is significant because powerful external factors come into play, affecting a child's academic and social success. Things that are out of the control of teachers have a critical influence on children's behavior and attitude toward life, school, and education.

Placing all of the responsibility for a child's achievement on the backs of teachers is not realistic. Responsibility should be shared among teachers, parents, and students. In addition, public policy affects the economic and social conditions of families. Poverty matters when it comes to education, just as affluence and family connections affect education and admittance to Ivy League schools.

We must be realistic about what teachers can and cannot control and design accountability strategies around those things that they have an ethical responsibility to control directly. We also lose sight of the fact that children grow and develop at different rates, and the impact of the teacher may not be observable immediately. If students are to receive a quality education, parents, teachers, and students all bear some responsibility. Whether each fulfills their responsibilities is critically important in creating a healthy foundation for kids.

Six external factors are critical in children's school performances. Berliner identified the following powerful factors: low birth weight and nongenetic influences; inadequate medical, vision, and dental care; food insecurity; environmental pollutants like lead and mercury; family relations; and neighborhood characteristics.[4]

Teachers are in control of the quality of their education and their preparation. They also control their

- ethical and responsible professional decisions;
- commitment, enthusiasm, and passion for their profession;
- desire to continue to grow and remain up-to-date on relevant research in their field;
- adherence to professional principles and conduct;
- individualization and differentiation of instruction to meet students' needs;
- classroom climate and discipline;
- interpersonal relationships with students, parents, and others;
- instructional rigor and techniques;
- use of time;
- creativity; and
- assessment methods for skills, thinking, concepts, and character.

ASSUMPTIONS, EVALUATION, AND CARROTS AND STICKS

Teachers, however, do not hold sway over some very important factors. These are not excuses, but realities. Teachers do not directly control or, in some cases, even leverage influence over

- parenting;
- family functionality;
- education of the parents;
- poverty;
- children's health;
- children's attitude toward education;
- peer group pressure;
- children's attendance at school;
- children's living conditions;
- drug abuse;
- parental philosophy and support; and
- home abuse.

Teachers do not work in isolation. The overall tenor of the school regarding safety, climate, culture, class size, curriculum, and operation is not in the direct purview of teachers. The culture of a school is important and sets the stage and tone for children's attitudes and behavior. School leadership and group commitment are interwoven in establishing a positive school culture and climate.

Teachers should be held professionally accountable for their performance. But holding them accountable when external conditions are beyond their control doesn't make sense ethically or professionally.

Professional accountability is complex. Assessing a teacher's individual performance on a single metric is irresponsible. The standard of care for children is important and is the responsibility of the teacher. That is something we can hold teachers accountable for, even though children may come from difficult social, economic, and family environments.

ESSENTIAL IDEAS TO REMEMBER

- Questioning assumptions is important in any effort to reform an institution.

- A difference exists between motivation and action based on force or fear.
- Mandates and regulations suppress creativity and innovation.
- Reliance on "carrots and sticks" runs counter to research.
- Context matters in evaluation and accountability systems.

NOTES

1. Jenny Anderson, "States Try to Fix Quirks in Teacher Evaluations," *New York Times*, February 19, 2012, www.nytimes.com/2012/02/20/education/states-address-problems-with-teacher-evaluations.html?ref=education&_r=0.

2. Larry Cuban, "Another Educated Guess about Philanthropy and Reform," blog, December 9, 2014, https://larrycuban.wordpress.com/2014/12/09/another-educated-guess-about-philanthropy-and-reform/.

3. Daniel Pink, *Drive: The Surprising Truth about What Motivates Us* (New York: Riverhead Books, 2009), 480.

4. David Berliner, "Poverty and Potential: Out-of-School Factors and School Success," Education Public Interest Center, 2009, http://nepc.colorado.edu/publication/poverty-and-potential.

Part II

Lifting the Fog

4

THE FOUNDATION

Public Education

> Knowledge—that is, education in its truest sense—is our best protection against unreasoning prejudice and panic-making fear, whether engendered by special interest, illiberal minorities or panic stricken leaders.—Franklin D. Roosevelt

During most of our lifetimes, public schools were seen as the bedrock of our nation and a source of pride for our communities: places to realize the "American Dream," where the playing field could be leveled and children could pursue their aspirations and have a life better than their parents.

The idea—uniquely American in many respects—was that it didn't matter where you came from, your nationality, who your parents were, or your socioeconomic status. What mattered was hard work and perseverance to learn and hone abilities and to face the future.

Free public schools nourished the concept that what you know matters more than who you know. Common people coupled with an education, talent, and drive could counter social status and elitist contacts based on wealth or position. Only in America is there a "Fanfare for the Common Man," instead of fanfares for some inherited royalty or elitist privilege. Public education celebrated the possibilities of the "common" citizenry.

During the last 40 years, however, public education has been under fire and targeted for reform. To some the perception of public education is that of a societal problem, not a cornerstone of our nation's future success. Once an avenue to a better future, education is seen by some today as a dead end that serves teachers and unions rather than children.

In actuality, public education has been one of the great pillars of our nation's rise to prominence. The United States survives politically, socially, and economically because of public schools. Approximately 90 percent of American children attend a public K–12 school; only 10 percent attend private schools. In many respects, public education is the backbone of our country. It has and will continue to shape our nation and society.

Today's reformers are at odds with history. Thomas Jefferson argued that locally controlled public schools were a key democratic institution. He believed that teaching children our political principles was essential to sustaining our form of government, and he advocated for local control of education so that citizens have the right to exercise self-rule on a matter of most importance to families.

John Adams in 1785 declared, "The whole people must take upon themselves the education of the whole people and be willing to have the expense of it. There should not be a district of one mile square without a school in it, not founded by a charitable individual, but maintained at public expense of the people themselves."[1] Adlai Stevenson, the presidential candidate in 1952 and 1956, stated that "the free public school system is the most American thing about America."[2]

By the end of the 19th century, Americans established and sustained a universal system of education that

- became the most decentralized system of school governance in the world;
- was controlled and financed locally and governed through majority rule; and that
- parents monitored in the interests of their children's education and future.

The United States embraced the principles of fairness and opportunity, which create a moral foundation for justice and equality.

The concept of universal public education rested on political and social ideals and shared political and social beliefs and democratic val-

THE FOUNDATION

ues. Values are powerful because they commit and sustain efforts over time to meet them. Honorable principles, like "all men are created equal" and "inalienable rights" continue as ideals that improve our government and society.

Horace Mann emphasized that teaching democratic values would produce a "civil society." Values such as individual responsibility, justice, equality, goodness, fairness, and democracy were considered part of the foundation of a child's education. Public education was the consistent and binding force emphasizing common values and principles. Character development was an imperative. This mission is greater than test prep, literacy, and job skills.

Support for public schools has been consistently high. The 2015 annual PDK/Gallup poll gauges and tracks attitudes toward public education. The results indicate high levels of support for public schools and a traditional view of where accountability should rest—state and local governments.

When asked what grade the individuals participating in this poll would give local public schools,

- 13 percent indicated an A;
- 38 percent indicated a B;
- 31 percent indicated a C;
- 9 percent indicated a D; and
- 4 percent indicated an F.[3]

Americans believe that their local public schools are better than other public schools across the country. Concerning public school nationally, 51 percent indicated that they deserve an A or B. However, 57 percent believe their local public schools rate and A or B.

Despite the reforms presented to provide vouchers, the poll found that

- 57 percent oppose vouchers;
- 31 percent favor them; and
- 12 percent don't know.

Concerning which level of government should hold schools accountable for what students learn, the poll participants indicated

- 19 percent favored the national government;
- 44 percent favored state government;
- 33 percent favored local government; and
- 4 percent didn't know.

Nationally, reformers are pushing for more testing. The results concerning testing indicate that 13 percent of those polled believe that tests are "not at all important"; 28 percent report that they are "not very important"; 43 percent indicate that tests are "somewhat important"; and only 14 percent consider them "very important."

The PDK poll results fly in the face of media opinion and the politicians and reformers who expound on public school failure and discontent. The impression they give is that parents are victimized and want privatization.

Local citizens and parents, in fact, can monitor local public schools and the school board. However, trying to get resolution from private sector organizations is much more difficult. If there are concerns, the citizen's voices are muted by legal means or corporate indifference. With public schools, local citizens have the means to express concerns and pursue procedures to seek justice.

The board of education is elected by the citizenry and is accountable to them. Corporate or foundation boards are not directly responsible to citizens and parents. Private boards do not have the transparency requirements for their meetings, decisions, or finances.

Public schools are not perfect. But no organizations are. Certainly, schools fall short at times due to funding, social conditions, distorted priorities, or poor leadership and teaching. Like all organizations, schools can be dysfunctional. But abandoning them and privatizing education would also destroy the ideals of upon which public education is founded, with no guarantee that the dysfunctions would evaporate or that decisions would be made ethically and democratically. Some private sector operations are testament to that.

Education is a public interest, not a private one. Public education is an idealistic institution. The mission of the school is to sustain our democracy through a citizenry that looks beyond themselves and cares for their communities and fellow citizens. Schools are to protect and empower citizens to participate in their own governance based on democratic ideals. These ideals—not marketplace priorities—should drive school change, the common good, and local school boards.

SCHOOL BOARDS AND THE COMMON GOOD

The U.S. Constitution delegates the responsibility for education to the states. States created departments of education and provided for the establishment of local school boards. The boards have been and should continue to be an important local governmental institution. After all, local governance and local boards are in close proximity to their constituents and can respond directly to citizens who have a vested interest in the schools and children's welfare. Centralized or private control of schools is against our foundational principles.

Public education is also publicly accountable: open meetings, transparent records, and the ability to seek judicial redress. At the state level, legislatures regulate academic expectations, personnel, standards, assessment, and certification. Local citizens and boards operate the schools; in that regard simple proximity makes them more accountable for creating and providing the best education possible for the boys and girls in neighborhood communities.

The debate about education is local, open, and transparent, something that would be more difficult if decisions were made in Washington, DC. No Child Left Behind and Race to the Top are testaments to that. Local control puts faces on accountability and emphasizes that parents, students, and educators are responsible for the community's children.

Local school boards, however, are not independent or isolated political bodies. They are responsible for adhering to the laws and regulations established by the state legislature and the state department of education. That said, having educational policy and practice determined by governmental bodies closest to the citizenry has always been a principle of American democracy, particularly for schools.

The recent transference of authority to the federal government for educational policy and practice through mandates and regulations is a relatively new trend. The concern and danger are having policies affecting children's education established far from local citizens affected by those policies. The legislative and executive branches of the federal government are difficult to influence by local citizens and are often willing apostles of lobbyists and big money interests.

In 1979, the U.S. Department of Education was signed into law with the mission to "establish policy for, administer and coordinate most federal assistance to education, collect data on U.S. schools, and to enforce federal education laws regarding privacy and civil rights." The mission of the department is "to promote student achievement and preparation for global competitiveness by fostering educational excellence and ensuring equal access." This mission, when applied in the political context, cuts deeper and has a significant impact, particularly when mandates and financial incentives are at stake.

Today, local school boards struggle with regulations, mandates, and finances. An open debate of issues can take place in each community. In the past, there seemed to be consensus regarding what schools were to be. Now, the national reform effort and the expectations it has established have raised questions and fears, including about the control, purpose, and future of public education.

The local board's role is making policy, where debate and discussion can take place. At the core of discussions are values, because policy is not value neutral. Change under any circumstance incites conflict, which in itself is not negative, but when strong consensus is not evident, individuals must demonstrate courage and fortitude to address issues and go on record. This is difficult when decisions are made in Washington or in private or corporate boardrooms.

LOCAL CONTEXT AND CONFLICT

What boards debate and how they do it indicates whether they are in touch with the essence of the school's purpose and soul. The focus of the debate defines their efficacy as a group. Discussing the issues in the form of dialogue generates understanding and better comprehension of the basic assumptions behind different options and the thinking and values behind them.

Dialogue allows people to think together and see divergent points of view and respectively consider options. Listening actively and clarifying for understanding are important in a productive dialogue.

Determining a collective vision for public schools requires open and respectful dialogue. Obviously one standard calls for "the best interests of the children" to be the determining factor. However, resources are not unlimited, local and political issues affect decisions, and when one is made, everyone may not be happy.

Board members must ask thoughtful questions and do their due diligence as part of their responsibilities to the citizenry. They must find common ground and positive connections in the school community by establishing clear values and principles under which they, administrators, and teachers operate.

Whether a school community is true to itself is a matter of integrity. To be a good steward of the school district, board members must ensure the honor of the schools by making their actions, words, and programs congruent with their core values and principles. All this presupposes the board and the community have a dialogue about the schools and the ideas under which they will operate. Dialogue on principles is positive and can instigate growth.

The common good through strong schools should be the board of education's primary focus. Citizenship emphasizes responsibilities and obligations. Service, responsibility, duty, and honor sound like anachronistic ideas from the past, but they are the mainstays of the common good and the sense of community that are necessary for society to work.

Communities are formed around values, ideals, and principles: the core that offers people a sense of identity and purpose. Communities are value based; politics is power based; and the private sector is profit based. The public has become cynical about government, which is a dangerous trend, particularly since younger generations repeatedly hear that government does not work and that it cannot be trusted. It does not work if special interests are served and the interests of the people are ignored.

The old adage that wisdom is knowing what you don't know applies to board members. Wise ones know what they need to learn. School districts are complex places fiscally, educationally, organizationally, and culturally. Board members need to understand the large and subtle issues of their school districts before taking action. New members must take time to sort out what they know and don't know. Grasping technical and policy questions takes time and work. There's a significant difference between opinion and knowledge, and information and understanding. Knowledge and understanding are prerequisites for responsible decision-making.

Good public servants understand what can be controlled and what cannot. Otherwise, policies and planning can be compromised. A local forum for debating educational issues is better than having bureaucrats or private sector interests make them. Stewardship and accountability are the foundations of public officials but are not necessarily at the forefront in the private sector.

The heart of stewardship is valuing what a school is and what it can mean to children. Board members must protect the soul of the school through a political process that has all the dark entrapments that can destroy schools and turn them into mere institutions, complete with standard operating procedures and no heart. To do that, communities must elect people with deep passion for children and with the courage to advocate for them. There is no greater public service than to improve the condition of children, who are powerless in the process of politics.

EFFECTIVE BOARDS: WHAT TO LOOK FOR

When examining local boards of education, there are several things that are significant, according to Mary Broderick, former president of the National School Boards Association.[4]

How well does the local board work with the superintendent of schools? That working relationship is extremely important to ensure that there is a clear vision of how the local schools should operate, as well as the nature of the programs and operation of the schools. At times local boards will not support an administrative proposal, but that does not mean that it does not support the leadership in a local district. An open and positive working relationship between the superintendent and the local board is absolutely essential.

The superintendent must also be cognizant of those values and principles when establishing appropriate educational practice based on quality research. Creating high quality organizations with ethical practice and age-appropriate standards of care for children is the role of superintendents.

Local boards have the major task of interpreting and sensing the will of the community and establishing educational policies that represent those values and principles. Policy questions should take the most time, and they should be debated because policy matters involve philosophical questions that interpret the essence of the school's soul and values.

Conflict surrounding these issues is not negative but necessary to achieve clarity of purpose and integrity. Conflict is not negative, if it is civil and if individuals are open to discourse. In many cases individuals are in agreement on values but in conflict over strategy.

The foundation for good policy rests on principles and values. They must be defined, and the debate should center on whether the principles and values are evident in the day-to-day life of the school and in people's relationships and interactions. Values are key because they define and distinguish school communities.

Successful boards consider a variety of perspectives and are respectful of individuals and do not shut people down. Listening is important and must be practiced in order to build credibility and confidence and to understand the content and intent of the public's input.

Civility is essential in any dialogue. The debate about education is essential, and the fact that individuals have different and conflicting values and proposals requires the boards to listen, respect all parties, and create a sense of trust. After listening to all sides of a proposal, local board members vote their conscience and then agree to support the collective board's decision, even though it may not be what the individual advocated.

In reality, successful boards want individuals within the system to feel safe to take risks and ask questions. Building pride in the system so that individuals present proposals in order to improve the system is important.

Local parents and citizens must inform the board of their issues and concerns and remind it that its actions are noticed in the bigger picture of children's lives in the local community. Getting others involved in a respectful way to talk about educational issues to board members is vital. When practices or policies are not serving children, parents and others have a responsibility to express themselves.

High expectations for the education of children are essential for boards, superintendents, principals, and the entire community. The questions asked must include the very basic issue of what constitutes a quality education for children so that they can lead meaningful and purposeful lives in the future.

STEWARDSHIP

Local school board members are stewards of the public schools. Stewardship rests on responsibility and a sense of the future. It is a far-reaching province of public officials. As citizens holding elective office, board members have a responsibility to take long-term care of the public schools and to protect the community's investment and the interests of children. They should leave the schools in better shape than they were prior to holding office. Making difficult and unpopular decisions today so the schools are better tomorrow is the role of a steward.

Stewards add value to the community rather than diminish it. Board members focused on their own self-interest in getting reelected can compromise stewardship for expediency and for their own popularity. Only in looking back do we recognize the public officials, from presidents to school board members, who have been good stewards.

Inquiry is not threatening. The board must ask questions and inquire into the principles behind proposals, the research base to support them, the rationale for initiatives, the costs, the expected results, and the accountability procedures to ensure proper implementation and outcomes. Sometimes educational and political decisions overlap, and local boards must be able to rise above local, state, or national politics to do what is best for children in their local community.

Stewardship requires courage to face special interests, the economically connected, the politically powerful, and the criticism of pundits and the press. Some board members and superintendents are cowardly lions in the face of economic, social, and political pressures. Doing what is expedient takes less courage than doing what is right. Decisions and pressure are a part of public life, but those decisions should look to the future and to the common good.

We must protect local schools because they are the only ones that are directly responsible for the needs of children in the community without any other agenda, motive, or special interests. The effort at privatization threatens parental and local control as well as transparency in decision making.

Running schools is not easy or always efficient. Democratic governance never is. But it's better than elites or corporations deciding the futures of our children and the education that they receive. Marketing is not results, and reformers are not always interested in the common good. Locally elected school boards epitomize what the founders believed. Democracy, while not perfect, is preferable to self-interest and control by the elites.

Public schools are an indispensable foundation of our democratic society. Keeping public schools democratic rather than agents of corporations or aristocratic politics is absolutely essential.

ESSENTIAL IDEAS TO REMEMBER

- Will private or corporate schools develop independent thinkers who will challenge authority?
- Are the values and purposes of these schools in harmony with Jefferson's and Adams's beliefs?
- The common good, not self-interest, is the driving force in determining what children should learn.
- Public education is a moral force for all children to pursue their talents and dreams and to directly participate politically and socially in our society.
- Through the decades, there has been consistent support locally for public schools.
- Local school boards make policy for local schools. They are more easily directed and controlled than Washington bureaucrats or schools run by private agencies and corporations.
- Stewardship is the basic role of school boards. They must act on values and principles for the common good of all children and ensure that they are upheld.
- Local dialogues about schools and education are generally healthy for communities and education.
- Democratic processes are superior to special interests or nontransparent privatized organizations.

NOTES

1. John Adams, "U.S. President Letter to John Jebb," 1785.
2. Sarah Mondale and Sara B. Patton, *School: The Story of American Education* (Boston: Beacon Press, 2001), 1.

3. "The 47th Annual PDK/Gallup Poll," *Phi Delta Kappan*, September 2015 (Bloomington, IN: PDK International).

4. Mary Broderick, personal interview, 2014.

5

EDUCATION OR SCHOOLING?

> Education is not filling of a bucket, but the lighting of a fire.—William Butler Yeats

The last 20 years or so have been a period of restructuring, reforming, reengineering, reprogramming, and reacting to find a solution to better schools. The solution may not rest in business and scientific management approaches but in the simplicity of a loving, creative, intelligent relationship between teacher and child.

Reforms have focused on schooling rather than educating. We tell children that grades, rank in class, competition, passing tests, and getting the numbers is all there is to becoming educated. As quantitative analysis drives education reform, we have lost our way. Reformers can be caught in the fog of a "hedgehog-ian" emphasis on quantitative measures and analytics that suggest that numbers equal an education.

By fixating on analytics, we lose sight of our mission and what's important in helping children. The emphasis on exam scores has narrowed the definition of education, driving out important aspects of children's learning. The supposition is that if children do well on standardized tests, then they will be well educated. But that assumption is wrong. Here's why.

The debate about public education raises a critical issue. Are students becoming well educated or well schooled? A fundamental difference exists: a significant one in determining the course of almost every other discussion about public education and efforts to improve it. Take a look at Wall Street, where individuals with degrees from highfaluting colleges and universities cooked books, reported deceptive metrics, and bilked investors and taxpayers. All of them passed standardized tests and demonstrated capability in reading, math, business, and finance. The question is: were they well educated or well schooled?

Look at Washington, DC. Many administrations are packed with the so-called best and brightest individuals with Ivy League law degrees and doctorates and demonstrating knowledge of content and concepts. The Kennedy, Johnson, Nixon, Reagan, Clinton, and both Bush administrations had smart people making foolish decisions—even unethical and illegal ones. The question is: were they well educated or well schooled?

In these examples, individuals work in complex and high-pressure situations calling for more than literacy and mastery of facts, concepts, and theories. Moreover, knowledge and facts are not static: they change over time as research, discoveries, experience, and perspectives dictate. All of us live in an increasingly complex world requiring more than "smarts" or "shrewdness." Schooling and diplomas are not sufficient evidence of being fully educated.

Philosopher Mortimer Adler suggested that being educated is more than finishing formal schooling. He stated that education is a lifelong process and not simply about passing tests or meeting graduation requirements. He stated:

> Those who are liberally trained to read and write, speak and listen, measure and calculate, have acquired the skills to go on learning after they have graduated, but unless they continue to learn year after year, they are likely never to become generally educated human beings. If the liberal training they receive in school includes a taste of all the major disciplines they will have some awareness of what there is to learn in order to become generally educated by the end of their lives. Becoming a generally educated person is a lifelong process.[1]

Knowledge is important but judicious reflection and understanding of the values governing its application is essential. Lifelong learning will not be enhanced by short-term exams. Decisions and behavior take more than information and knowledge; they require foresight and a sense of wisdom.

WISDOM: A BLAST FROM THE PAST

Wisdom is a term seldom heard today, and it has become almost anachronistic when discussing education or reform. Why?

Being intelligent is not synonymous with being wise. Wisdom is not the regurgitation of facts, and it certainly is not a competitive activity. While wise people have a broad and deep background of information and knowledge, there's a distinction between being smart and being wise. Wisdom is more difficult to acquire than encyclopedic knowledge, and it is more than a strictly cognitive exercise.

Wisdom has multiple facets, both intellectual and philosophical. In the Harvard study of adult development, George Vaillant identified the following qualities of wise people:

- maturity to empathize
- common sense and moral discernment
- appreciation of context
- intelligence to get to the heart of matters
- emotional intelligence demonstrating care and justice[2]

Wisdom grows out of the heart and the intellect, which is a big difference between schooling and education. There are many historical examples of people who had impressive academic credentials but who acted in uncivilized and brutish ways. Cognitive ability, although important, is not sufficient. Wisdom involves moral understanding, heart, spirit.

Historically, there were individuals who "had the paper"—degrees—from prestigious universities. Although they had the diplomas, they lacked an ethical framework to govern their life and decisions. Although well schooled, they made vile and immoral decisions that injured people and were destructive to society. Principles perished and values vanished. History highlights the importance of being educated, not just being schooled.

Josef Goebbels received a doctoral degree in humanities from prestigious Heidelberg University. Yet he went on to run Hitler's propaganda machine that led to the deception and destruction of millions of people across Europe. Empathy and morality vanished into heartless madness. Although he was well schooled and had academic knowledge, he acted without nobility, virtue, and wisdom. He could pass academic tests but failed ethics and humanity. Unfortunately, he is not an isolated example.

Contrast Goebbels with Dr. Albert Schweitzer. Schweitzer also received advanced academic degrees but had the strength of character to combine his head with his heart and to contribute to improving the lot of humanity. Goebbels and Schweitzer are two highly schooled and highly credentialed people who used their information and knowledge for dramatically different purposes due to the nature of their character and the content of their hearts.

Schweitzer was educated and wise; Goebbels was smart and schooled. If recitation of content was the prime criterion, then the Internet, computer, or other technical system could be considered well educated. The application of knowledge requires more than cognition and efficient plans and processes.

Wisdom requires the information and knowledge necessary to reach understanding, but a reservoir of information and knowledge does not result in wisdom. Wisdom requires the intelligent application of knowledge coupled with deep insight into what is ethical and virtuous. Wisdom concerns moral and ethical frameworks and the principled use of knowledge.

Bill O'Brien, CEO of Hanover Insurance Company and founding member of the board of governors of the MIT Center for Organizational Learning, believed that wisdom is more than intelligence and the mastery of content. He stated, "it suggests a special quality of judgment in human affairs based on knowledge of moral principles, human nature, human needs, and human values. Wisdom is more than what people know; it is who they have become, and who they have become as determined by how congruent their behavior is with their knowledge. It is not enough for leaders to know moral principles—to have credibility as leaders and thus to earn followership, they must live up to their knowledge."[3]

O'Brien speaks directly to leadership, which is pertinent to everyone. Children must understand that all citizens and people have moral responsibilities that require much more than regurgitation of facts, figures, and concepts.

Though we can pass a test of knowledge, can we pass the test of an honorable life rich in humanity, character, and behavior? To be truly educated, core philosophies must be developed and pursued both personally and professionally. Application of knowledge, skills, and content through wise decisions elevates the lives of individuals and their communities.

Wise people discern the inner qualities and essentials of relationships and are astute enough to see the subtle nuances of the impact of knowledge on people, relationships, and society. They are able to weld knowledge with compassion, integrity, imagination, and hope.

Elementary and secondary education can help children prepare for the future with a broad education and thinking skills, but it also requires perspective on values and standards of thought and behavior. The comment about the Whiz Kids—smart but not wise—applies here. Education is much more than "smartness."

To acquire wisdom, children need to meld their hearts and intellects with principles and character. The only test for character and honor is in the exercise of life and its challenges. Knowing and reciting principles is different from having the courage to live them, which demands moral sense and dedication beyond self-interest. Intellect is the only thing schools seem to measure, except when coaches talk of the "heart" their athletic teams demonstrate on the playing field.

We all want children to move beyond facts and figures and become "good" people who fuse knowledge and thinking with character and values and who exemplify righteous behavior. Even though the motives and goals are the same, children's behavior may be different because of the wonderful uniqueness of each child. Some children are more reserved and others more flamboyant because of the nature of their personalities. However, their actions or behavior can be equally noble and wise in living ethically and with meaning in their individual lives and as a citizen.

THE GAME OF SCHOOLING

"Anyone who truly cares about children must be repelled by the insistence on ranking them, rating them, and labeling them. Tests do not measure the sum and substance of any child. The tests do not measure character, spirit, heart, soul, potential. When overused and misused, when attached to high-stakes, the tests stifle the very creativity and ingenuity that our society needs most. Creativity and ingenuity stubbornly resist standardization."[4] High stakes test pressure destroys initiative for learning and turns students off from school.

Appropriate skill tests are helpful in assisting teachers in making sound instructional decisions for a class or for individual students. But one-time, high-stakes test events compromise time for creative and imaginative lessons that promote reasoning and higher order thinking skills. Developing healthy skepticism is important. Doing the difficult spadework of thinking, discussing, and challenging takes time and patience.

We are teaching students the "game of schooling" as if it were a short-term competitive exercise—do what you must to pass, get a diploma, and get out. Teaching that competition is the only approach to reaching excellence, as if principles, commitment, and hard work do not matter, is erroneous. In school we teach that there are haves and have-nots. This all flies in the face of the very concept of learning—lifelong learning.

The great philosophical questions of life—truth, beauty, justice, liberty, equality, and goodness—cannot be assessed by a computer-scored test. Searching for answers to these issues is at the very core of our society and the essence of becoming well educated. These great ideas should be studied in school and understood by our children if they are to live a life of depth, understanding, and principle.

All of our children, rich and poor, can contribute to the common good, be responsible and active citizens, and adapt to changing times. Thinking critically, posing questions as well as seeking answers, and understanding and developing an ethical and moral framework are a part of being well educated, which isn't easy to gauge on a multiple-choice instrument or to explain in a simple sentence.

Unfortunately, some of our schools are becoming too narrowly focused, and our competitive society has pushed some of our high school students to the point where they feel that they have to cheat in order to get ahead. Cleverness, cunning, and cutting ethical corners are not standards of an educated person. "Greed is good" is a destructive notion that destroys credibility, ensures cynicism, and eventually wears at the soul. Celebrity is a poisonous concept that is vacant and shallow and sometimes self-destructive.

Imagination, joy, ingenuity, wonder, and idealism must not be wrung from our schools. These ideas separate American education from that of other countries, and they are the basis for a well-educated and civil society. They are also key components to our political and economic systems. These intangibles are the foundation of the success of our children and our country.

ESSENTIAL IDEAS TO REMEMBER

- A difference exists between being well educated and well schooled.
- Working toward wisdom is the goal of a good education.
- Wisdom requires lifelong and continuous learning and development.
- Students should study and think about the great philosophical questions and begin to understand the moral and ethical responsibilities that they have to their families and society.

NOTES

1. Mortimer J. Adler, "Adler on Education," www.catholiceducation.org/en/education/catholic-contributions/adler-on-education.html.

2. George E. Vaillant, *Aging Well* (Boston: Little Brown and Company, 2002), 253.

3. William J. O'Brien, *Character at Work* (New York: Paulist Press, 2008), 96.

4. Diane Ravitch, *Reign of Error* (New York: Alfred A. Knopf, 2013), 241.

6

WHAT IS AN EDUCATED PERSON?

> It is the mark of an educated mind to be able to entertain a thought without accepting it.—Aristotle

The United States is the only nation that officially refers to "pursuit of happiness" as a value. There are no guarantees of happiness, just one's ability to pursue it. Public education exists so that each individual has the perspective and ability to engage in the pursuit.

Pursuing happiness and fulfillment requires more than academic knowledge. This search for education certainly involves academics and the arts, but it extends beyond content knowledge mastery.

In actuality, the real search, for all of us, is to discover ourselves: our talents, passion, joy—our path in life. An education has a spiritual dimension, not in the religious sense, but an understanding of our total selves. It involves mindfulness and an awareness of our relationship to nature in the world, our relationship to others, and our relationship to ourselves. This is broader than cognitive content and entails really knowing who we are so that we can authentically pursue those things that are in harmony with our heart and soul as well as our minds.

Schools must provide an environment in which children can discover themselves and find their strengths and passions. They should discover their uniqueness but also see the connections they have to the world, society, and others. An education should help children find what wants to emerge from inside of them. No test can do this—although they can stymie the pursuit. Children find their passions and what their work and life is: their mission and purpose.

Being educated has three areas of emphasis. Educated people have the capacity to see with new eyes. Their minds are open and they see and perceive what is unfolding in the world and society with a fresh perspective. They are mindful and aware of the integration of issues and what is unfolding. Their minds are not closed but pursue and explore new ideas without filtering out new and innovative concepts.

In all of this, education broadens us; we realize that we gain things but that we also have to let go of things. Importantly, we have to let new perspectives and ideas come to us. An education opens us to the future and to what is emerging and does not cement us to the past. Listening, perceiving, and understanding connections in our lives are important for us to continue to learn and adapt.

Being educated moves beyond simply understanding events or concepts; knowing our connection to those outside of us is important. Empathy and compassion are important. An open mind and open heart involve the intersection of knowledge with responsibilities and obligations to ourselves, others, and community.

Educated people have the capacity to sense and shape their futures. They don't bounce to and from issues and crises. Schools, in many cases, teach rote, dot-to-dot ways geared toward short-term exams. What is required, particularly in an unfolding and uncertain future, is creativity supported by continuous intellectual curiosity, which is necessary to shape—not simply to react—to the future. Our children need to be educated to understand their responsibility in a democratic society and to gain historical perspective about their duties to their family, community, and country.

One way to squander creativity and intellectual curiosity is to "make sure that educational policies like high stakes testing (No Child Left Behind) and other methods guarantee for years to come that teachers cannot create an environment that allows our children to experience and explore their deeper levels of awareness, creativity, and knowing."[1]

We don't know what the future holds, but we do know that change is inevitably a large part of it. In that regard, children need to open "their minds, hearts, and intentions"[2] to cope with what emerges in the future. This is more than skills. Anyone 50 years or older today can testify to the fact that conditions are vastly different than they were 30 years ago. Consequently, we have to educate students in ways that avoid making their education or their employment capacity obsolete or irrelevant.

In this regard, students need to be self-reflective about knowledge and how they relate to it. Simply regurgitating content is not the answer, but determining how knowledge relates to principles and values in their own view of their life takes a higher measure.

The future and how we think about it is important. Hierarchical power or market competition is not necessarily the path to finding success and happiness, nor are they effective. The future rests on individuals. Scharmer stated, "every human being is not one but two. One is the person who we have become through the journey of the past. The other is the dormant being of the future we could become through our forward journey."[3]

Education concerns continuous learning and contemplation. Being well-educated means having a sense of stewardship and a concern for the common good, not simply tending to self-interest and ego needs. Well-educated people revere knowledge and apply values and principles to guide them as they pursue a meaningful life of purpose. They try to make wise decisions premised on strong ethical and moral ideals and broad academic understanding.

Certainly strong academic skills are important, but so are values and principles that form the foundation for their life's decisions. They ask questions. They are skeptics, not sheep. They engage civically and stand on principle. Philosophy and wisdom are essential in becoming self-reflective and personally and socially conscious.

All of us have had to confront issues and change in our lives. Change is the consequence of creativity, conflict, and innovation. Intellectual skills are more than literacy and numeracy. They involve the ability to get information and to organize it and to define the values that undergird arguments. Being educated means articulating and synthesizing ideas clearly and logically and formulating new perspectives. Being able to analyze, synthesize, and evaluate issues, concepts, and information are essential. In addition, defining issues and problems and questioning assumptions are necessary in all facets of our lives.

A basic requirement of education is an understanding of the ideals and values surrounding the concepts of democracy, liberty, justice, equality, beauty, and goodness. Discerning the truth and seeing through distortions, self interests, and unethical use of data and information are essential. Being skeptical is fundamental to being a critical thinker and an active employee and citizen.

In essence, all children need a strong liberal arts education. Specialization and narrowing their education is a disservice not only to them, but also to our society in the long run. Problem solving involves a broad perspective across content and a deep understanding of the principles and moral expectations required to maintain and create a civil society.

Exploring ethical principles and their relevance to historical and current circumstances is necessary in an ever-changing world. Students should study rhetoric so that they learn to appreciate language, persuasion, and dialogue. Appreciating literature and the fine arts is essential because they enhance creative interpretation and the application of concepts, principles, and culture. They should also grasp quantitative reasoning and its advantages and pitfalls, particularly in this age of STEM (science, technology, engineering, and mathematics). Children learn to use deductive and inductive reasoning but also to apply intuition and passion.

History has demonstrated that in totalitarian regimes, the first classes to be restricted and jailed are the artists, writers, poets, and philosophers. The fine arts are not "add-on" or extracurricular activities. They are basic to becoming educated. Understanding cultural values and their philosophical foundations are necessary for ethical and moral decision making and conduct.

EDUCATION AND FRENCH HORNS

In symphonies of almost any era, the French horn, as a solo instrument, exemplifies nobility and heroism: its characteristic strong, mellow tone tugs at the heart and spirit and increases the pulse rate.

Metaphorically, the same should be true of schools. They are about nobility and hope. Nobility is a matter of the heart and soul, and the heart is the home of hope and integrity. The arts exemplify this.

Leon Botstein, in his book *Jefferson's Children*, stated:

> The arts create and sustain new ways of keeping freedom from losing meaning. They help individuals retain their own sense of uniqueness in a world in which the pressure to conform is intense. They fill out the hollow structures of democratic rights with meaning that is profoundly personalized. It provides an imaginative world in which each individual can find a place and effectively fight the battle against

deadening conformity. They are not superfluous embellishments of life, the ornaments we can do without. Like science, the making and appreciating of art is integral to the practice of freedom. The arts challenge the monopoly of commerce in matters of fundamental values. The many generations of philosophers who have pondered integral relationship between beauty and truth, between aesthetics and ethics, have done so with extremely good reason.[4]

Ironically, many learning experiences with little apparent practical value are essential to understanding the human condition and our ability to function as successful human beings. Is there room for a discussion and an understanding of beauty? What about the concepts of liberty and justice, which are continually being redefined? Is a great piece of literature or a poem of little use in boardrooms, factories, or law offices? Does peeking into the soul of an author for an intimate glimpse of the heart and spirit of humanity create greater meaning and an understanding of harmony, joy, and imagination? Education must go beyond preparing children to merely work and exist: it helps them live.

Education should be a French horn that appeals to children's hopes and dreams, which can be played in a variety of tempos, keys, and moods. It's not simply an exercise in obtaining a job, basic literacy, filling out applications, or getting into a college of choice. Education is not always pragmatic, and its sole objective is not the acquisition of material goods and employment opportunities. Nobility in human conduct comes from people who have reached beyond skills and basic information—those who have moved beyond ego to ideals and principled character.

Children need to hear French horns calling them to higher levels and ideals of education and life and to continue their pursuit of happiness. Appreciating human genius, imagination, and creativity—even in the pursuit of things that are viewed as impractical—should be honored. Educated or well schooled: the fate of all of us depends on the difference.

21ST CENTURY SKILLS?

Change was consistent throughout the 20th century and every century before that. Humankind progressed and will continue to do so, albeit through different modes and paces. A calendar change doesn't mean that education must change dramatically.

People born in 1911 experienced technological advances during their entire lives: film, radio, telephone, television, computers, flight, and a host of others. They experienced Henry Ford's assembly line production, as well as a man landing on the moon. Their lifetimes were filled with social changes (voting and civil rights), economic depressions and upturns, international conflicts and wars, civil rights movements, and growth and global development of business and commerce.

Certainly children today will see changes we cannot even fathom. Many of us will not be around in 2050, but our children and grandchildren will. So what are the learning needs of our four-year-old grandchildren that will enable them to pursue happiness?

Change is a constant, always has been, and always will be. In fact, from an economic standpoint, company life spans are much shorter than that of people. In his book *The Living Company*, Arie de Geus indicates that the life span of Fortune 500 or equivalent companies is between 40 and 50 years.[5] He states that companies that survive have a "sensitivity to the environment" and the ability to learn and adapt. The same is true for our children and for us.

When all is said and done, children today need a strong education that includes thinking and problem solving and personal skills and concepts. Children need self-awareness in order to understand concepts in all major content areas. Ethical and philosophical concepts actually may be more critical and essential as scientific and technological advances occur.

Philosophy and ethics, especially in times of change, become central issues in decision making as new innovations challenge the status quo. All children need to see the implications of ethical decisions—theirs and others'. That is basic in times of change. Otherwise their lives, businesses, and the country can spin out of control.

What is the definition of an educated person who can thrive and succeed in changing times in any century? Children need knowledge and wisdom supported by content and skills to adapt and resiliently face continuous change.

A WORD ABOUT TRAINING VERSUS EDUCATION

Training is aimed at proficiency in an art, a profession, or a job by being able to do something in a particular way and to a certain standard. In other words, training is the practical application of particular skills.

Education is a prerequisite for training. Training is not a substitute for education. It's a short-term folly to get a second-rate education and try to go through a first-rate training program that requires strong educational and learning skills like problem solving and the ability to work alone or to cooperate in teams. Educational skills are essential and required for training programs, and individuals without them will not be able to be trained today or in the future. Today's training can be tomorrow's shackles as innovation continues to progress and alter our lives.

Training today for specific jobs is a precarious proposition. What jobs will be available in 2040? What skills will be necessary? One has only to look back 40 years to see the difference in jobs then and now. Getting a good education is really the best bet for employment in a nebulous future: it prepares individuals for training as well as for other aspects of life besides employment. After all, there's more to living a "good" life than a job. A comprehensive education is the best approach.

The fact is that children need strong educational skills and insight, whether bound for college or for technical training. The need is greater today than at any other time in the past. A liberal arts high school program is the most practical education of all. Education should celebrate human genius, explore great ideas, and create a foundation so that wisdom can grow with the times. Being trainable is more important for the future than is specific job training for today.

FORMAL AND HIDDEN CURRICULUM

For children today, it's what happens tomorrow morning—not what takes place in the future—that is most critical. Children live in the present, and their daily experience is what counts. But each day there are two curricula at work in schools. The first is the written, adopted official program, and the other is the social experience of school, the hidden curriculum.

To the layperson, curriculum reform seems simple—establish goals and standards for reading, writing, arithmetic, and a list of other content areas and classes. Usually, the curriculum is a big document that defines what should be taught, when it should be introduced, in what grade and in what sequence, using what materials, and for what length of time. How to assess student learning also is spelled out.

The formal curriculum, which is adopted by the school board and becomes the policy of the district, is supposed to be implemented by the teachers at each grade level. It is linear and sequentially defined by grade. The assumption is that if children experience the whole program, they will learn everything that is essential for them to become educated.

School districts assess the goals, objectives, and experiences in the official curriculum and report the progress of students to parents and the community usually through test accountability. Nice and tidy—but there are problems.

Just because it is officially adopted doesn't mean that the curriculum is going to be fully or consistently implemented. Scores of programs exist on paper but never see the light of a classroom. There are reasons for this. Some teachers disagree with the program and close the curriculum guide as fast as they shut their classroom doors. Others resist the rigidity of enforced teaching methods and lost autonomy and originality, in addition to the specter of wrongheaded teacher evaluations.

Although there are problems with the official curriculum, the hidden curriculum has great potency because children feel and experience it every minute they are in school. This curriculum concerns the students' relationships and social interactions. Though not written or adopted by the board, it is readily apparent to students. The hidden curriculum is a critical part of a student's daily education as they interact, from kindergarten through twelfth grade, in the place called school.

The hidden curriculum impacts children's perceptions of themselves and their relationships with people. While the official curriculum deals with content, the hidden curriculum involves intent—the effects of the school and classroom on children. The official curriculum concerns doing; the hidden curriculum is about being. The official curriculum is written, while the hidden one is experienced.

The hidden curriculum is value laden and affects the norms of interaction between children and teachers, adults, and peers. In all schools, children are a part of a crowd. Children face power and social divisions in schools. Power comes in the form of teacher control, as well as from the scrutiny of peers. Teachers obviously must make judgments about students regarding their behavior or work. These verdicts are sometimes made publicly, and all of them connote value: what is good and acceptable and what is bad and unacceptable.

When adults evaluate students, they reinforce values about what is judged and how it is assessed. In this role, teachers dole out plaudits and rebuffs. The children who are "good" are granted privileges, which means they comply with the teacher's instructions and directives. The others face redirection or other consequences.

Students also evaluate other students; they are both subjects of evaluation and participants. In this day of social media, the impact is stronger. Peer scrutiny carries tremendous weight and impact affecting the self-judgment of each child and his or her sense of self-worth and belonging. The judgments of peers either mean inclusion or exclusion: acceptance, rejection, or worse—indifference. High stakes for a person of any age. Children's worth is determined in part by their approval as a peer, their performance as a student, or their level of docility or compliance in the face of authority.

The hidden curriculum differentiates between the weak and the powerful. Peer judgment about the value of an individual child can be made on the basis of performance: which students meet expectations and which do not. The cliques evident in schools betray the workings of the hidden curriculum as students associate or separate themselves from others. They categorize themselves in a number of ways: jocks, academics, nerds, artsies, techies, and others. Some groups have more clout than others and get greater recognition and reward from students and teachers.

The norms and expectations of the hidden curriculum come to bear on children every day, giving rise to the following issues:

- What effect does hidden curriculum have on the student's dignity?
- Does the hidden curriculum respect all children equally or are some valued more than others?

- Is there a gender difference in how the hidden curriculum affects children as reflected in the attitudes of teachers, counselors, or students themselves?
- What do children learn about the exercise of power and authority in social settings?
- What do children learn about democratic values from experiencing school?
- What do children learn about fairness and justice from the hidden curriculum?
- What is the definition of goodness in the hidden curriculum?

Conflicts sometimes exist between the hidden and the official curricula: they can be at odds with each other, contradicting the adopted word with visible practice.

A goal of the formal curriculum is to encourage students to be curious and lifelong learners. Yet in many schools, curiosity becomes a serious problem as students drift off task, take precious time with too many questions, or explore topics not in sequence with the "real" program. Another example is the "official" expectation that students will be active participants and contributors, though, in reality, many classrooms expect and reward docility.

Children who stand up for their beliefs can experience negative repercussions from teachers who think that the students are refuting authority or from peers who worship on the altar of conformity. As another example, the formal program may celebrate independent thinkers, when in practice many teachers or social groups expect children to be conformers, to check their creativity and imagination at the door, and to "stay within the lines."

The hidden curriculum does not have a formal assessment process of tests and measurements, but it does have a communal one that children either meet or don't and are rewarded or sanctioned. This assessment is not always objective because the hidden curriculum is a place where subjectivity thrives.

In implementing or monitoring the official curriculum or acting out the hidden curriculum, the role of teachers is central. They make judgments based on the performance or behavior of children and then implement a program based on that assessment. In effect, children are measured against the mold discussed earlier, and those who fit it are rewarded and those who do not, fail. To many people, school is expected to sort people into the categories and roles they will inhabit as adults. The hidden curriculum, however, sorts and defines children on different terms than the standards of the official curriculum.

The slicing and dicing of children becomes destructive in developing them as people and in increasing their academic performance because individuals live up or down to expectations. Teachers in schools that operate on the basis of soul and values look at children differently. In these schools, teachers are moral agents who consider the interests of their children first and do not discriminate on irrelevant grounds. They act on clear values that are consistent with the school's purpose and soul.

When teachers act as moral agents, they act with virtue. They are polestars. They are not simply disseminators of information and knowledge: television, computers, and books can do that. Their responsibility is greater and rests on their obligation as professionals to go beyond the technical aspects of their jobs as designers of lessons, classroom managers, or curriculum implementers.

Teachers are nurturers, not sorters, of children, helping them to meet their potential by developing talent. Modest talent connected to intense drive and energy can produce great things. Teachers need to be aware of both their blatant and subtle impact on children's motivation, desire, and spirit. They care for the spirit within children, in addition to tending to matters of the intellect.

ESSENTIAL IDEAS TO REMEMBER

- Educated people have open minds and hearts and are able to adapt to what is emerging in the future.
- Being educated requires deep knowledge and cognitive and affective concepts and skills that include complex thinking, academics, and the fine arts.
- Philosophy and ethics are important in becoming educated and pursuing happiness.
- Children confront formal and hidden curricula, both of which have an impact on their learning and self-concept.
- Training and education are two different but interrelated ideas.

- The fine arts are essential to becoming fully educated. They are not "add-on" or extracurricular activities.

NOTES

1. Otto C. Scharmer, *Theory U: Leading from the Future As It Emerges* (Cambridge, MA: Society for Organizational Learning, 2007), 299–300.
2. Scharmer, *Theory U*, 447.
3. Scharmer, *Theory U*, 401.
4. Leon Botstein, *Jefferson's Children: Education and the Promise of American Culture* (New York: Doubleday, 1997), 223.
5. Arie de Geus, *The Living Company* (Boston: Harvard Business School Press, 1997), 6.

7

LEADERSHIP AND ACCOUNTABILITY

> Leaders push through the fog of uncertainty and build bridges to success, even when the path seems clear.—Unknown

Life emerges in mysterious and engaging ways, providing challenges and opportunities. Sometimes it is harsh or tender, noble or crass, or quiet or bombastic. If our lives were flat lines with no peaks or valleys, leadership would not be necessary, and there would be little poetry in the nature of things.

Leaders, particularly teachers, impact others' lives. They toil in the messy fields of day-to-day life, the clash of reality and principle, and the emotional heat of heart and soul. Leaders live in intimate relationship with the minds, hearts, and souls of people, and they touch us in ways that help us see the world and ourselves more clearly and sometimes through a different lens. The metaphors leaders use affect how people perceive the truth in creating a shared vision.

Life is not an exercise in micromanagement; it does not follow a logical or sequential path and it is filled with whimsy and mystery. Events occur due to serendipity and synchronicity, immune to statistical analysis. The unanticipated in life frequently hands us the biggest challenges, the largest gifts, and the greatest satisfaction. Plans are impotent because our lives and destiny take unexpected turns.

Rationality is not always supreme. Life is unpredictable, more poetic than scientific: it is not simply about "doing"; it is about who we are as beings. We all face yearning for belonging and for finding our calling.

We usually think of our life in an external way, examining what is outside of ourselves as if bystanders to a play unfolding around us. We think the context is out there in the greater world, as if we exist solely in social, political, and economic circumstances. But there are strange attractors within us that are more powerful than external forces or expectations guiding us in finding meaning. Our metaphors define our perspective of reality and how we structure our lives.

Outer and inner forces, tangible and intangible, affect our personal and leadership behavior. The unseen world of unquantifiable intangibles creates challenges. In this respect, leadership is not an emotionless endeavor: it connects with the character and heartstrings of people and stimulates insight and inspiration. Leaders engage in conversations about high ideals and righteous causes and how our lives at work can be rewarding and fulfilling.

Leading has a moral dimension requiring that ends and means have the same harmonic structure in both our internal and external lives. Great leaders call on our better angels and summon us to use our imaginative energy and human determination to act with virtue and goodness.

Our institutions and their leadership rest on credibility, which is the coin of leadership. Without it, leaders become nothing more than vacuous symbols of power and deceit. When trust dissipates, the grip of cynicism and apathy increases.

The 2012 Leadership Index Survey found that 69 percent of Americans believe that we are in a leadership crisis. Worth noting is that these polling results pertain not only to the usual bogeymen of American institutions such as large corporations and Wall Street. Americans remained rather proud of some institutions, such as the nation's schools, until rather recently: "confidence and sectors [institutions] that are critical to the nation's strength and strategic direction remains abysmally low. . . . Educational leadership, so important to the country's future competitive strength, continues to languish in fifth place from the bottom, among the sectors for whom Americans have 'not much' confidence."[1]

Untrustworthy leaders cannot challenge others to greatness. Truthfulness matters. Serving the public is really about serving the citizens of our democracy. Hard truth matters. Leaders with moral courage tell people what they need to know, not what they want to hear. Defining moments for leaders revolve around issues requiring moral courage.

Leaders create cynicism when their words raise our spirits but then act in ways that are totally alien. We hear of noble ideas and then experience bankrupt procedures and policies, devoid of coherence and principle. We hear the bugle call of great goals and experience paucity of resolve or bogus sincerity. We hunger for realness and substance in our leaders and are disappointed when we observe obfuscation and shallow posturing. We yearn for relationships built on trust and straight talk and tire when they dissolve into condescension and glibness.

The promise we seek in leaders falls on the barren soil of ego and arrogance, as some lack the courage to admit failure or to learn from it. Unfortunately in life we experience "bad" leadership that has implications for costs and mission, as well as relationships with employees and the public.[2] Bad leadership emanates from ethical breaches or incompetence.

Ethically corrupt leaders lie, cheat, or steal. Others are simply uncaring, unkind, or oblivious to the needs and desires of others. A subtler area is insular leaders who minimize or disregard the welfare of those outside the group or the organization they lead.

Bad leadership also stems from lack of competence—the skill and ability to institute effective action and strategies to sustain positive change. Some of this is caused by leader rigidity and failure to adapt to new ideas and changing times. In some cases, incompetence arises because the leader lacks self-control, which inhibits or destroys relationships.

With bad leadership, followers are not off the hook. They have an obligation to pay attention, to be skeptical of leaders and their so-called mission. Questioning assumptions and motives is a prerequisite for proper analysis and action. With today's reform efforts, we must do the same. People should take a stand and challenge proposals and policies. Taking action against unethical conduct is essential in order to avoid becoming a silent accomplice. Not to do so is itself an unethical act.

With challenges facing public education, good leadership is an imperative. Leaders can be polestars for appropriate value-based behavior because of their interests in the common good, not ego, profit, or power. Leaders can do several things to ensure "good" leadership. First, having a culture of openness to new ideas is essential. Having strong and independent advisors and associates who are willing to "speak truth to power" are valuable and necessary instigators of positive conflict.

Getting people to coalesce around a common objective in a complex socio-emotional-political-economic environment takes more than orders and procedures. Deep commitment is not born out of data and analysis. Data and information do not have the power to capture people, to have them serve and commit their talent, or to have them dedicate their lives.

People want more than computer printouts, graphs, regression analyses, and tests of statistical significance. Dee Hock, the father of the universal Visa credit card said, "We are now at the point in time when the ability to receive, utilize, store, and transmit data—the lowest cognitive form—has expanded literally beyond comprehension. Understanding and wisdom are largely forgotten as we struggle under than avalanche of data and information."[3]

Hock warned that we are drowning in a flood of data and information and that "the raft of wisdom to which we desperately cling is breaking up beneath us." He went on to warn that "if we fish for absolutes in seas of uncertainty, all we catch are doubts."[4] People yearn to live lives of significance. Wisdom and relationships really matter.

Reaching for noble ideals beyond metrics nourishes us inside and outside and fuels our passion to serve something greater than ourselves. "Doings," management processes, and expectations can be learned. "Being"—authentically and honestly—is another thing.

The vein of gold in leadership is about who we are authentically as leaders, which is important when serving children and building credibility with parents and others. Our being speaks louder than our words because it has to do with integrity to values and principles. Being is about genuineness, truth, and essence, not about style and appearances.

Being has to do with character and forming a bond with others. People want leaders who are committed, honest, competent, inspiring, and forward looking. Leaders live these traits consistently, not sporadically or when they think it works to their advantage. True leaders demonstrate loyalty and respect and pursue their ethical duties consistently, building trust and confidence.

In fact, even the military emphasizes leadership as "being." The army's view of leadership is "be, know, act": "There are three aspects to leadership regardless of organizational level or military rank: who you are inside, what you know, and how you act."[5]

Being is not tied to having things or titles but is about who we are, which allows us to take risks and endure criticism during hard times without the fear of losing position or power. Playing roles is not genuine or authentic. Who leaders are on the inside inevitably becomes visible over time. Service, honor, respect, and sense of duty are anchors that communicate more than management skills.

LISTENING ACTIVELY

To lead, leaders must know themselves. They must understand their intentions, their fears, and their needs. Otherwise, they are simply playing a role in deference to others. A leader's "being" speaks louder than his or her "doings." Authenticity comes not from titles and roles, but from internal character and understanding.

Being reflective is important for leaders. They must review the past and their experience. Self-understanding and reflection is necessary for leaders to create a vision and lead into the future.

Reflection requires listening on a number of different levels.[6] First, leaders must listen to the echoes of the past and use what they learn to evaluate and synthesize current issues and events. The present, however, is not a clone of the past. Other things are necessary.

The present challenges leaders to examine the issues and reconfirm or discount prior—"old"—judgments and opinions, ensuring that they do not live in the past or pursue tried-but-not-true approaches. Without this, leaders can blindly move into a morass of difficulty based on being married to former times.

Leaders must also listen to outsiders with an open mind. Noticing differences between today and the past "good old days" liberates thinking. An open mind is not stuck in the past, nor is it a prisoner to experience. Current forces and issues should unlock new analyses, opportunities, and direction—if there is openness to the present.

In all of this, quality leaders are empathetic and try to see through the eyes of others. Lack of empathy can exacerbate a difficult and destructive position and cause false analyses through analyzing the situation with wrongheaded statistics.

Too many times scientific managers look at data and discount the underlying feelings and emotions in what is happening and emerging. Leaders must lead from within: examining the role that emotion plays in events and responses.

Leadership vision really comes from using knowledge, emotional understanding, and intuition to connect with what is becoming manifest in the future. Sensing the shifts that are taking place is necessary in order to let go of old ideas and allow new ones to blossom.

Listening is not a passive activity. Though it may not be physically active, it is anything but passive within our hearts and minds. New ideas coupled with valid ones from the past generate new perspectives and allow us to come together with a fresh vision congruent with our moral imperative.

Leaders lead with the head and heart and will to make a difference and be successful in an emerging future.[7] This includes operating not from a hierarchical or market-driven approach, but through networks and collaborative systems so that new solutions that serve the common good can be created.

Many perceive leadership as a matter of control and power. Others see power as the energy of potential, commitment, and thought. Relationships, not processes, spur creativity and help people fulfill themselves at work. Relationships that capture people's passion for great causes and commitment are a true act of leadership.

AT THE HEART OF LEADERSHIP

Leaders have the huge task of transforming individual talent and potential into a collective performance. Certainly competence, skills, and concepts are important, but there is more.

Fred Kofman, in his book *Conscious Business* stated, "consciousness is the ability to experience reality, to be aware of our inner and outer worlds. It allows us to adapt to our environment and to act to promote our lives."[8] Leaders must reflect on their positions and why they hold them so that they behave authentically and "be" the role of leader. Understanding their own feelings and motivation is important if they are to act with principle and honesty.

Only when leaders understand themselves can they help others develop their potential and self-actualize in their roles. Teachers, in particular, are in their profession to find meaning by helping children to grow and learn. "Self-actualizing work transcends ego, freeing people from an exclusive preoccupation with themselves," and helps people find gratification beyond self-interest.[9]

Conscious leaders use their knowledge but also their intuition and feelings. Disequilibrium flows around us and is inevitable at times in our personal and organizational lives. We are not simply technocrats trying to engineer commitment and change in a rational, sequential universe. Logic and data influence behavior and outcomes, but they are not enough. We have all been bitten by so-called data that was inaccurate, wrongly focused, or simply deficient.

Peter Senge wrote, "People with high levels of personal mastery do not set out to integrate reason and intuition. Rather, they achieve it naturally—as a byproduct of their commitments to use all the resources at their disposal. They cannot afford to choose between reason and intuition, or head or heart, any more than they would choose to walk on one leg or see with one eye."[10] We must better understand the concrete, emotional, and abstract aspects of our relationships, environment, and reality.

Emotions are always a part of life, and leaders who are emotionally distant generally cannot connect with or understand people. Indifferent rationality can be tone-deaf and can destroy a leader's credibility, no matter how intelligent he or she is. Leaders cannot help people without compassion and cannot right wrongs without emotional fervor and indignation.

Heart is always mentioned in discussions of great leaders because it drives focus and commitment. Leaders are passionate and committed to serve. Their hearts direct them to do what is honorable in the face of jeopardy and commit them to great causes when logic and odds may dictate otherwise. Heart causes leaders to lead by outrage when injustice and tyranny are present.

Discussing heart and intangibles does not mean that strong leadership or organizational accountability is lacking. Accountability does not rest strictly on metrics and quantification. Qualitative approaches are also important. But accountability has been made unnecessarily complicated. When accountability relies on simple concepts like Bics and broccoli, it becomes understandable.

BICS, BROCCOLI, AND ACCOUNTABILITY

What do a Bic lighter and a stalk of broccoli have to do with accountability for today's schools? What would you do if your superintendent said that that he or she was going to structure schools like broccoli and function like a Bic lighter? You'd probably call the school attorney and have him or her committed. Sounds crazy, but these two disparate items hold the keys to high functioning, accountable schools—or other organizations, for that matter.

Accountability is one of the great political buzzwords of the day, and one of the biggest issues facing school leaders and boards of education. Presidents Bush and Obama both touted the need for accountability in education. The question is not "why accountability?" The question is "what kind of accountability system makes sense?" That's where Bics and broccoli come in.

Accountability has two facets. A primary one is the obvious question about whether the school district and its students are achieving at high levels. The second is whether school programs, operations, and procedures have integrity. Sometimes this second issue, which is essential, gets overlooked.

Schools are accountable for what they accomplish: the outcomes and products of the system. They are also accountable for the processes and procedures that are used to achieve the outcomes: how things get accomplished. These two purposes are what Bics and broccoli are all about.

Bic lighters, along with a few other products and services, have four simple characteristics:

1. They do what they say they do.
2. They do it consistently over time. They do not perform to high levels occasionally, or spike once and decline, or do it only for a select population.
3. They do it under all conditions.
4. They do it cost effectively.

So Bic lighters do what they were supposed to do consistently, under all conditions, and for less than $2. School districts should aspire to the same characteristics. For parents looking for quality schools, asking the following questions can be revealing.

Does the School System Do What the Mission, Values, and Ethics Say It Does?

In finding a quality school, parents must first determine what the school indicates it is going to do to educate your child. All schools are not the same. Programs differ. To determine the answer to this question, the school program and the nature of its curriculum, instruction, and assessment must be examined, as well as a statement of its values, goals, and mission.

Does the System Perform to High Levels Consistently over Time?

Consistent performance concerns two things: it means that high achievement and performance levels are not one-time events, demonstrated on only one measure, or with a small sample of students. High performance is demonstrated over time, not just one quarter, semester, or year. The level of performance is evident in several measures: culture, climate, work product, performance, test results, or creativity. Any quantitative comparisons must be statistically and ethically sound.

How Does the School Determine Success?

Achievement cannot rely solely on multiple-choice tests. It includes student work product: written essays, research papers, and stories; debate and speech, drama, and performance; question and response; research and project completion. Character and behavior are visible demonstrations of values, concepts, and ethics.

Does the System Perform to High Levels for All Children, Regardless of Socioeconomics, Race, Family Demographics, or Other Factors?

This question is an important one. High performing schools not only demonstrate high achievement over a long period of time, but students from various demographics—social, economic, racial, and ethnic backgrounds—also do well. There are not huge achievement gaps between students, and student success is consistent over time. This is a difficult criterion to meet, since children come from diverse backgrounds, some of which have great influence on whether they are successful in school.

High quality schools do not make excuses but work with students as they come to the schoolhouse door. Students of the same chronological age are not necessarily of the same cognitive, emotional, social, or physical age. Schools take this into account, and teachers and others work with them so that they can reach their full potential. Longitudinal studies can be valuable because the impact of teachers and a school is not always immediate but can be very significant.

Is the System Cost Effective?

A Bic lighter is cost effective, doing its job for about $2. A quality education should be cost effective. Education isn't cheap, but it can be cost effective. Where and how school districts spend the money is important. The primary focus of school spending should be on teaching and learning. Schools are large and complex businesses. Ensuring that there is proper management of a school or school district is essential to spending finite funds cost effectively.

Cost effectiveness is not cheapness. It is about the results achieved for the dollar spent. In the vernacular, it is "bang for the buck." Programs that do not achieve high results for the dollar spent may be robbing themselves of the opportunity to try new ideas or to fund cost-effective ones.

So what does broccoli have to do with all of this? Examine broccoli closely. Each small piece is reflective of the whole. They look the same; they are fractals. Ferns and cauliflower are also examples. In science, fractals are complex patterns created through simple processes operating over and over again.

Concerning the issue of quality, organizations should look like broccoli, meaning each department, level, school, and staff supports the four principles of quality. If they do, then a total organizational culture of quality is created. Following simple principles and values allows for autonomy as long as the process and programs are in harmony with them. The whole organization has credibility and ethical patterns of operation. In other words, if each department acts with integrity, then the entire organization will model those values.

Bics and broccoli provides simple concepts that promote accountability of both process and outcomes. Straightforward, clear principles coupled with commitment from all individuals can produce an accountability system not based on one-dimensional or ethically questionable approaches.

Quality schools have integrity—honesty of purpose. Values, effort, and performance are linked and congruent. High achievement in academics and ethical and responsible behavior are priorities, coupled with a structure that promotes caring, equity, and commitment. Quality schools are innovative and flexible and create a climate in which children can learn and be creative.

Comprehensive outcomes, not just those aimed at basic skills or standardized test results, are characteristics of quality schools. They include intellectual, academic, character, citizenship, and interpersonal, social, physical, and cultural goals. They assess children's performance in a variety of ways not tied to tests or other simplistic measures. They also examine their integrity and credibility in meeting their mission and values.

Finally, school leadership does not rest in one position, but exists between and among all professional and support staff. Leaders are competent, credible professionals who set clear goals and model values. They are genuine and authentic in their feelings and have established the trust necessary for people to be creative and innovative. Power is perceived as energy, not control or a matter of carrots and sticks.

ESSENTIAL IDEAS TO REMEMBER

- Leadership is not a mechanical act. It involves a complex mix of authenticity, heart, values, competence, and relationships in the pursuit of a noble goal.
- Leadership is not simply about "doing." Its foundation is the "being" of the leader—his or her character, integrity, and honesty in words and deeds.
- Leaders must know themselves. Playing a role is not leading.
- Accountability rests on whether organizations do what they say they do consistently, over time, with all students, and cost effectively.

NOTES

1. Barbara Kellerman, *Bad Leadership* (Boston: Harvard Business School Press, 2004), 235–37.

2. Kellerman, *Bad Leadership*, 235–37.

3. Dee Hock, *The Birth of the Chaordic Age* (San Francisco: Berrett-Koehler, 1999), 224.

4. Hock, *The Birth of the Chaordic Age*, 225.

5. Leader to Leader Institute, *Be-Know-Act: Leadership the Army Way* (San Francisco: Jossey-Bass, 2004), 8.

6. Otto C. Scharmer, *Theory U: Leading from the Future As It Emerges* (Cambridge, MA: Society for Organizational Learning, 2007), 11–13.

7. Fred Kofman, *Conscious Business* (Boulder, CO: Sounds True, 2006), 3.

8. Kofman, *Conscious Business*, 281.

9. Kofman, *Conscious Business*, 281.

10. Peter Senge, *The Fifth Discipline: The Art & Practice of the Learning Organization* (New York: Doubleday, 2006), 157.

8

POLESTARS, PARENTS, AND PUPILS

> In teaching you cannot see the fruit of a day's work. It is invisible and remains so, maybe for 20 years.—Jacques Barzun

Many of our lives would not be as rich and full without the fair-minded guidance, patience, discipline, and nurturing of our teachers. Their sage advice rings in our ears for decades, and their mentoring and modeling support and reinforce us during easy as well as difficult times.

Life isn't like the movies, where revelations happen instantly and heroically; it's more subtle than that. Sometimes significant moments reveal themselves when we pause and think back. Retrospect reveals powerful and significant moments and relationships.

The connection between student and teacher is not assessed easily or demonstrated in statistics. The relationship is not simply cognitive: it really rests in the heart and spirit and awakens self-discovery and optimism.

Teachers are critical anchors that help, support, and provide direction. Children have to work through the developmental stages of growth, face the socioeconomic realities of their families, find their place in the world, and confront their insecurities and uncertainties.

Remember the teacher who pulled you aside and made you feel worthwhile and more than simply another student in class? The one who saw the virtue in you and understood the fear and uncertainty that you felt? The one who helped you to see the goodness in yourself and the potential lying dormant inside of you?

Sometimes teachers helped us by telling us in caring and poignant ways difficult things we didn't want to hear but needed to confront that made a difference. These connections are the bonds and times we recall when we think about who we are and how we got here. The intangibles of a significant relationship with a teacher live forever because they were individuals who were authentic and trustworthy.

Teaching is about relationships, not about procedures or practices. Computer avatars can be programmed to follow routines of lesson design and implementation, but they cannot feel or deal with students who come to school with varying emotional, social, and philosophical perspectives and needs. Simply instituting a process does not address children's needs nor does it encompass a teacher's role.

Teaching is not a robotic act: it is much more complicated. Genuine human connection between people cannot be manufactured simply by implementing strategies. Empathy, compassion, and patience are keys that allow students to invest in a teacher's guidance. That relationship is unique. One teacher may be significant to one child but may not have the same effect on others. Children differ and significant relationships are individualized.

The spark of motivation burns at different levels of intensity and at different times. We all know children who didn't do well in school, but who, years later, earned advanced degrees, became entrepreneurs, or found themselves as successful lawyers, physicians, entertainers, business owners, or teachers. Their lives and accomplishments superseded, with the help of teachers and other mentors, the projections of what they might achieve based on their behavior and performance in school. Their potential and maturity did not develop in isolation, but evolved in their own time and with the guidance of teachers. Life doesn't have a statistical scoreboard.

Trust and understanding anchor the relationship between students and teachers. In reality, there are no quick fixes to academic or emotional growth. Judgments made from standardized tests may actually do damage to children whose potential can be unlocked only over time. They are not receptacles of facts and figures, but individuals with imperceptible potential and talent that tangibly blossoms through a credible and genuine relationship with a teacher.

As Einstein said, "it is the supreme art of the teacher to awaken joy in creative expression and knowledge."[1] The art of teaching creates relationships that inspire students never to settle for anything less than their best. Talent and creativity take time to evolve. Without compassionate and patient support and a safe environment to try, fail, and succeed, children aren't able to find their paths.

Teachers are principled role models who are demanding and ethical. Children feel safe to be themselves with them and are not afraid to take on new challenges because they trust their teacher. There are no algorithms for creating significant people, interactions, or relationships that impart wisdom. Relationships are not matters of statistical probability; they are human interactions complete with foibles, serendipity, and emotion that cannot be planned to occur at a particular time, place, or pattern.

Memorable moments develop because the timing and context are just right. Significant relationships actually set the stage for the successful application of the science of teaching because the doors of trust and confidence open. Without that significant relationship with a teacher, a focus on learning may not take place at all.

When asked about significant teachers who made a difference in their lives, people highlight factors about the quality and nature of the connection they had with the teacher and the teacher's character. Listening and understanding make a difference, as do challenging and encouraging. Raising questions opens the doors of introspection and motivation. Mutual trust is built on these and creates the solder of significance.

Great teachers believe in the inherent goodness of the children under their care and provide a positive example. They provide a reliable and firm guiding hand and never give up on children. Students' needs come first. A sense of humor and joy in working together softens doubt and struggle. Genuineness matters in connecting with children. Playing a role is far different from being in an authentic relationship.

Evaluating teachers and measuring significance is not easy. The depth of a human relationship is beyond measure. Teachers have an impact apart from their "doings" of implementing best practices. Human beings have intellect but also heart that clarifies issues and directs their behavior. They sense the feelings and attitudes of others.

Reformers propose a measurable teacher accountability system and a better brand of teachers as a solution to improved schools. As a consequence, reform plans center on teacher performance assessment based in significant part on standardized or so-called value-added test scores.

Newsweek in its March 2010 cover story entitled "Why We Must Fire Teachers" concluded that teachers are the problem with public education. Michelle Rhee, featured on the cover of *Time* magazine in November 2008, posed with a broom to "clean house" and fire teachers as a solution to better education. "Waiting for Superman," a film by Davis Guggenheim, places teachers and teacher unions at the core of educational problems. These vehicles disregard the social context of schools, the needs of children from impoverished backgrounds and neighborhoods, and the lack of funding and support for schools and children, respectively. The simplistic answer always seems to be that quantitative measures gauge effectiveness and significance.

The notion is that if teachers follow "best practices," high achievement will follow. The assumption is that best practice equals higher scores, which equals best teachers. The conjecture undergirding this approach is that if teachers would just follow the script and regimen, they will be effective teachers.

Teaching skills of lesson design and implementation is far easier than awakening heart and passion. Authenticity and genuineness are not programmed, rehearsed actions. Great teachers are comfortable in their skin and reflect a personality and style unique to them. Through the variety of personalities and commitment to quality practice, individual students find a human connection—a mentor, a role model—who can help them see themselves clearly and utilize their potential. Understanding how to work with children so that they can fulfill themselves, find meaning and purpose, and a sense of wisdom cannot be reduced to a Hollywood script.

Great teachers appreciate both the art and science of teaching in building constructive and compassionate relationships. None of us would be where we are without those teachers. We shouldn't forget that.

TEACHERS AS CREATIVE ARTISTS

Teachers are like artists—poets and musicians—who deal with important ideas and concepts and matters of the heart and soul. They are creative technically and interpersonally.

Artists speak of mind, soul, and spirit—life itself: its purpose, wonder, beauty, and travails. They help us think of ourselves with respect to others and the universe and highlight the marvel of life in bright or dark times. They define humanity and dream of noble ventures and the simple beauty of nature and human tenderness.

Great teachers do the same for their students. Rallying them through insight and wisdom, they unlock motivation within their students. Character and honor make a difference in life's path. Helping students reach for a higher calling has always been a teacher's ideal. Teachers and artists help us to see the world and ourselves more clearly and maybe with a different perspective. They frame and highlight the stark and tender realities we face in life.

Both teachers and artists work the soil of intangibles—those immeasurable things in life that are hard to measure but that make us uniquely human and alive. Teaching is not an emotionless endeavor: teachers connect with the heartstrings of children, not just their minds. Insight and motivation result because of their attachment.

Teachers help us find "where we ought to be" in life, our place and calling in an ever-changing world where things fit and feel just right. Finding that place doesn't always come easy or fit with the expectations of parents or others. It's an individual journey all must take.

Good artists and teachers invoke both wonder and a range of emotions when they share their truth through strong, positive relationships and experiences. This involves exploring together the great philosophical questions that we all confront in life: what is truth, beauty, justice, liberty, equality, and goodness?

Finally, life is the proverbial journey complete with crossroads and occasional dead ends. It does not always follow a methodical or sequential path but is filled with serendipity and synchronicity. The unanticipated in life frequently hands us the biggest challenges, the largest gifts, and the greatest satisfaction.

Teachers celebrate life by helping children face their yearning for belonging and finding their calling in pursuit of their ambitions for a good and happy life. Poetry helps all of us to live with and understand the mystery of life and our humanity, and music raises and stirs our souls. Teachers can be significant poets in our lives.

Teachers are truly significant virtuosos: those "polestars"—mentors—who make deep, substantial connections with students and guide them intellectually, morally, and emotionally. The art of teaching may have the biggest and longest-lasting impact on students' lives. After all, who remembers strategies? We remember people. We remember feelings. We remember character. All children need teachers who can touch their spirits, excite their minds, and ignite the fire of motivation.

Passion for working with children and the art of teaching are essential for a deep bond. Without passion, what is left are instructional and management processes. We have all experienced people who are technically proficient but "tone-deaf" when it comes to relating to people. Actually and unfortunately we see this also in other professions like law, medicine, politics, as well as education and others.

Deep understanding of child development, skill in improvising and customizing instruction, and authenticity in working relationships with students are important. Transforming knowledge into passion and zeal attracts students and awakens their curiosity and commitment. Great artists make music for the spirit and soul. So do great teachers.

STUDENTS AND PARENTS: THE HARD TRUTH

Much of the focus of school reform has been on teachers, but what about students and parents? The bond between parents and children is primary and supersedes all other connections. It can be either positive or negative. Parents and students both have responsibilities and obligations if children are to be successful in school.

When it comes to education, we have deceived our children. Not intentionally, but because we care for them and want them to avoid pain and difficulty of any sort. So we soft-pedal the fact that getting an education is not always going to be fun, that it's not going to be easy, and that, in some cases, it might be difficult, not physically, but in facing the hard work and inconvenience necessary to learn.

We know this because we had to face it, but we also know that education and wisdom just don't fall out of a tree—they require dedication and commitment. Children need to learn this, and it is their duty to do so.

American philosopher Mortimer Adler addressed the issue of getting an education directly. He said:

> Anyone who has done any thinking, even a little bit, knows that it is painful. It is hard work—in fact the very hardest that human beings are ever called upon to do. It is fatiguing, not refreshing. If allowed to follow the path of least resistance, no one would ever think. To make boys and girls, or men and women, think—and through thinking really undergo the transformation of learning—educational agencies of every sort must work against the grain, not with it. Far from trying to make the whole process painless from beginning to end, we must promise them the pleasure of achievement as a reward to be reached only through travail. I am not here concerned with the oratory that may have to be employed to persuade Americans that wisdom is a greater good than wealth, and hence worthy of greater effort. I am only insisting that there is no royal road, and that our present educational policies, in adult education especially, are fraudulent. We are pretending to give them something which is described in the advertising as very valuable, but which we promise they can get at almost no expense to them.
>
> Not only must we honestly announce that pain and work are the irremovable and irreducible accompaniments of genuine learning, not only must we leave entertainment to the entertainers and make education a task and not a game, but we must have no fears about what is "over the public's head." Whoever passes by what is over his head condemns his head to its present low altitude; for nothing can elevate a mind except what is over its head; and that elevation is not accomplished by capillary attraction, but only by the hard work of climbing up the ropes, with sore hands and aching muscles. The school system which caters to the median child, or worse, to the lower half of the class; the lecturer before adults—and they are legion—who talks down to his audience; the radio or television program which tries to hit the lowest common denominator of popular receptivity—all these defeat the prime purpose of education by taking people as they are and leaving them just there.[2]

Sounds old-fashioned, doesn't it? But in today's world of television, computers, iPads, and other technology, being constantly entertained is a vast aberration of real life. Easy ways are not always the best ways, and life cannot be reduced to cartoons, pseudo-educational games, and snippets of YouTube, which require no effort, much less reading or writing. Certainly technology is a resource, but it is not a panacea or a way to avoid the hard work of thinking and learning. Although video games may exercise the child's thumbs, they do not necessarily exercise their minds or their ability to think skeptically, critically, or deeply.

Learning is hard work that requires commitment. Teachers are not entertainers. In the old days, many of us were taught that we must work hard and that our lives will be better because opportunities will avail themselves. No simple three-point plan or a quick pill will instill an understanding of knowledge, concepts, values, and responsibility. Education and the hard work to get there is empowering and a part of the lesson.

In the past, students were expected to get the most out of school. Parents from all socioeconomic backgrounds valued education and its importance in the long haul of life. They held their children responsible and would not tolerate today's claptrap that students are not responsible for their poor grades, attendance, or behavior and that the teachers are at blame.

Life isn't always easy: difficulty, unfairness, and harshness exist. Our welfare and future can be threatened. Tough patches arise, and how we respond is very important. The same is true for children growing up. As much as we may desire, we cannot protect and shelter our children from life and tough situations.

What we can do is teach our children that they are not helpless and hapless victims. There are things they can do when confronted with challenging times. They have options, and their decisions are important. They are able to respond during troublesome times and situations. They are response-*able*.

Many current reforms place all of the responsibility for children's achievement on the shoulders of teachers, thinking that teachers are the most important factor in children getting an education. That's overly simplistic and negates any responsibility of parents and students for learning and achievement.

In a sense, many reformers place parents and students in the category of ill-fated victims at the mercy of others. First, parents' responsibility is to prepare children for school; second, children are responsible for their conduct and learning with each increasing grade.

The straightforward fact is that parents and students have duties and responsibilities. Both are response-able. Neither are simply victims; both are active participants in the process of education.

During conflict or harsh situations, there are two ways to approach the circumstances. Some individuals assume the posture and mentality of victims: awash on the waves of circumstance, victimized by forces beyond their control. They flail and curse at the state of affairs and toss their hands up in frustration. They go through periods of rejecting the conditions and hoping things will change. Blaming is a prime indication of victimhood.

Victims believe that the only recourse in life is to accept impotence, that they are not able to respond and meet their obligations. Self-pity, a woe-is-me attitude, and a lack of responsibility characterize victim mentalities. Hoping that circumstances were different does not change things, and cursing the darkness does not bring light.

Certainly, students face situations that challenge their competence, reputation, and status. Victims explain to others that the fault is not theirs and deflect any personal accountability, as if they were oblivious to what was happening. Maybe they are not fully culpable. Maybe there are better ways to address or manage the situation. Taking the position of no responsibility for what transpires puts them into the class of victim. We see this more frequently in our society, and it's extremely destructive.

Two levels of responsibility exist here. First, was the individual through actions or benign neglect answerable for the events that led to the situation? It does not mean that he or she did anything ethically wrong or was incompetent. Maybe the problem was not recognized, the wrong approaches or strategies were applied, or the desired results were not achieved. Not examining one's role in the situation leaves only the position of hapless casualty. We are seldom benign or irrelevant in events in which we were a party.

The second responsibility concerns the actions the individual took once the situation was evident. Was there a better way to address the situation and become an active player? If not, what approach could be taken besides blaming others? Unfortunately, sometimes, "it is what it is"—wishing things were different is futile and a waste of time. Sometimes, circumstances just happen.

Active participants take responsibility and accept circumstances. They accept conditions as they are and do not engage in fantasies of the cavalry bugling their way over the hill to save the day for them. Instead, they see reality for what it is and take action. They are not victims.

Being responsible for one's conduct and obligations is essential in our society. Too often, people avoid, deflect, or ignore responsibilities and justify their conduct as a result of victimization by others or society. Certainly there are inequities and injustices. But some people try to excuse their behavior and do not want to be held responsible, even when unfairness does not exist.

Children are not immune from that syndrome, and parents in some cases foster or even encourage it. The whiny three year old who manipulates parents to get what he or she wants, the adolescent who blames his or her behavior on peers, high schoolers who point the finger at teachers for their own poor grades—all of these are means of deflecting personal responsibility.

We do not do students a favor by diffusing or ignoring their irresponsible conduct. Today, poor performance in school seems to be the teacher's fault. Conflict with police officers is the fault of the officer on the beat. Failure to stand up for principle is the fault of the system or the expectation of others. Failure to meet obligations is because ... (fill in the excuse).

For a successful society and a rewarding life, meeting duties is a prerequisite. Being responsible personally and socially has a moral and ethical dimension. Being responsible is a part of citizenship and dealing with ambiguity and change. Assuming responsibility is a part of being successful in any line of work and a necessity to being a good friend and neighbor.

Parents must be responsible. Children need direction and correction. Without teaching children their obligations and the importance of meeting them, we are handicapping their future to live with integrity. Excuses do not matter and eventually erode character and credibility. They do not need excuses—and they can be participants, not victims.

Participants do not look through the rearview mirror and live in the past. They move ahead, looking through the front windshield to address the situation for the best possible outcome. Taking responsibility means addressing the situation and using talents to meet needs and requirements to the greatest extent possible. Responsible people contribute and have a role in determining outcomes and events, and will at least be a factor in the conditions and circumstances surrounding a possible resolution. Although it may not result in total resolution, a mature person works toward a conclusion, even if it means leaving the circumstances entirely. Sometimes we just have to admit that we were wrong, apologize, and move forward.

Responsible participant or victim? This distinction is not intended to diminish hurt and turmoil, and it does not ignore the fact that injustices occur or that fairness gets trampled in political pastures. These things occur. The issue is how we respond to the circumstances. Being a responsible participant provides a sense of efficacy, the ability to respond, which is a personally powerful position. Another issue can get in children's way—"specialness."

DISABLING SPECIALNESS

Specialness is ego driven. It separates, not unites us. By definition not everyone can be special, so if we are special, then others are not.

Look at our society. We are enthralled with royalty: is there really a divine right of kings? Magazines are dedicated to celebrities, which today does not necessarily mean talented or intelligent people, just outrageous or narcissistically outspoken. We even have television shows focusing on so-called idols. Idol worship is garishly inappropriate in a country that supposedly embraces "Fanfare for the Common Man" and believes that all people are created equal.

Children are unique. Uniqueness is multidimensional. It's more than a linguistic distinction—it's a real difference in how we look at ourselves and how we perceive others.

Children have to understand that they are unique and one of a kind—but so is everyone else. Uniqueness celebrates the individualistic character of the human race while "specialness" separates. Honoring individuals for their uniqueness is part of the American dream. In a way, we are all connected by our uniqueness—our talent, perspective, personality, appearance and character.

Amid the continual drumbeat telling children that they are special, we can easily become a nation of narcissists who need the admiration of others and look externally for their sense of worth. They become ego driven and focused on "what's in it for me?"

The article "Are 'Millennials' Deluded Narcissists" discusses the American Freshman Survey. For the past 47 years, the survey has been given to thousands of college freshmen. The article indicates that more students than ever consider themselves gifted and 80 percent rank their "drive to succeed" above average. In other words, the students feel pretty special about themselves, which the article stipulates can lead to a sense of entitlement.

Uniqueness is not having your picture on the cover of a monthly magazine Oprah style. When people die, it's interesting that we remember their character, idiosyncrasies and foibles, and their relationships and passions—the uniqueness of their distinctiveness.

In the final analysis, our uniqueness unites us as one-of-a-kind human beings who will never be duplicated. Our children deserve more than the hollow goals of fame, applause, or ego salving. They need to know that they matter and have the unique ability to respond and create a life that is personally fulfilling, and so does everyone else.

HARD TRUTH FOR PARENTS

We all know that teachers are important in helping children to learn and in creating an appropriate climate for that to happen. Some reformers have misinterpreted research to indicate that teachers are the most important individuals in helping children succeed in school. That's not entirely true.

Research suggests that, among school-related factors, teachers matter most. The key words are *school-related*. Children's lives do not start in school. They begin at home. Frequently overlooked is the fact that parents are critical factors in children's success at school. Parenting is one constant from birth through elementary and secondary school that affects the attitude, commitment, and performance.

Too frequently, the media focus only on schools, seemingly taking parents off the hook for their children's behavior and performance in school. The research, however, is very clear: students do better academically and socially when their parents are actively involved in their education. Positive attitudes toward education, reading to children at early ages, and consistent, positive discussions with children result in better attendance, increased motivation, lower rates of suspension, fewer instances of misbehavior, and better grades and graduation rates.

When parents believe that getting an education is important, it has a positive impact on children's attitudes toward school. This cuts across all socioeconomic standings of families. Parents, regardless of their socioeconomic backgrounds, can have an impact by supporting schools, teachers, and the important work of getting an education. There's no excuse for parents not laying the solid groundwork and positive attitude toward getting an education and being constructively involved in school. Time is required—that's all.

Parents who value learning, self-discipline, and hard work establish expectations for achievement and encourage reading, writing, and discussions at home. All it takes is time. Commitment from fathers, mothers, and grandparents to establish routines and monitor out-of-school activities such as television and computer time sends a message to children. Creating a home environment that encourages learning and communication and establishing reasonable expectations for children can produce positive results. No excuse is valid for parents not becoming involved at school by attending school functions, communicating with teachers and principals, and raising issues of concern.

Children with parents involved in their schooling are more likely to have higher grades, better social skills, and adapt well to school. Parental support for teachers, encouraging children to do their best, and providing encouragement and support are important for all children. In reality, there is no excuse for parents not to do this, because it does not require money, just focus and commitment.

Apathetic parents, disengaged parents, helicopter parents, overly protective parents, absentee parents, or abusive parents create problems for their children, making it more difficult for them to focus on academics and to respond positively emotionally, physically, and intellectually. The truth is that factors at home and outside of school have a major impact on what goes on at school. We understand this with mature adults in their work life, and we should certainly understand this with children.

Parents or grandparents can support children in school. This has worked for generations in the past. Value education and educated people. Children need to know that parents appreciate education, as well as their teachers and other educated people who have an impact on them. Children value what parents value.

Parenting is not always easy. The schools may be able to help. Finding support during difficult times helps both parent and child. Value education and demonstrate that to your youngsters. If they see that you value it, then they will, too, and will strive for the best education possible so that they can pursue their dreams.

ESSENTIAL IDEAS TO REMEMBER

- Being a significant teacher—a polestar—is not a mechanical or technical act. Although processes and procedures are valuable, teachers become significant because of the intangibles that go into a trusting and helping relationship.
- In reality, significant teachers are artists who understand and apply methods and techniques to create a deep, personal, and important relationship with children.
- We should not teach or encourage students to accept a victim mentality, which can be debilitating and destructive for them.
- Parents have the most significant role concerning children's attitude toward education. They must provide an environment that supports education and teachers and that reinforces children's responsibility and obligation to become educated.

NOTES

1. Alice Calaprice, ed., *The New Quotable Einstein* (Princeton, NJ: Princeton University Press, 2005), 70.
2. Mortimer J. Adler, *Reforming Education: The Opening of the American Mind* (New York: Collier Books, 1941), 234–35.

9

THE SOUL OF SCHOOLS

> The essence of community, its heart and soul, is the non-monetary exchange of values; things we do and share because we care for others, and for the good of the place.—Dee Hock

Schools are not like other organizations or bureaucracies. The needs of schoolchildren are different from those of workers in private industry or other organizations. Sure, there are business, asset, and financial aspects of schools that support the school's mission, but the mission is far more than profit and loss margins.

Children are not miniature adults. Applying workplace practices to schools is an imperfect fit. First of all, a school's mission is bigger than pushing for profit and producing goods and services. Schools are about spirit and relationships and the common good. In that sense, it is individualized, not standardized. The contrasts between schools and the private sector or other organizations reveal notable differences.

"In the race for the rational, the scientific, and the measurable, we have lost sight of something more important—an ecology in which work serves people, not only as a means for earning a living, but also as a platform on which we can develop our talents and express our best selves. The soul of an organization concerns more than matters of the bottom line," according to Bill O'Brien.[1]

In *Good Business*, Mihaly Csikszentmihalyi says, "Perhaps the best way to explain what the word 'soul' connotes is that, no matter how complex a system is, we judge it as having no soul if all its energies are devoted merely to keeping itself alive and growing. We attribute soul to those entities that use some portion of their energy not only for their own sake, but to make contact with other beings and care for them."[2]

O'Brien goes on to say that leaders must love the people with whom they work. He adds, "we have to understand what love is. Love is not limited to romance, family, and friends, but extends to every human endeavor, including the conduct of commerce. By 'love' I mean a predisposition towards helping another person to become complete."[3] This is exactly what teachers do.

Teachers have always had a deep sense about who they are, what they care about, and what they believe in. They, more than employees in other organizations, use the word "love." We've all heard teachers say, "I love children. That's why I'm a teacher." Finding purpose and meaning in caring for children who require understanding and nurturing is a force stronger than profit or self-interest.

Schools are organizations in which you hear the word love without reservation or fear of ridicule. They have a sense of soul, not in a religious sense, but in regard to mission and purpose and the commitment they inspire working together for the common good.

Teachers demonstrate love by committing themselves to children so that they can live a life of purpose. Loving kids is not a platitude; it's part of the personal and professional lives of teachers and should be inherent in schools. Caring begins with listening, understanding, and accepting, which evolves into deepening appreciation and, ultimately, love.

In an organization with soul, there's a connection between an individual's inner life and external aspirations. That's why O'Brien and Csikszentmihalyi see organizations as more than spreadsheets of expenditures and profit. Both advocate that helping people fulfill themselves in their work is an act of love. "The companies that survive longest are the ones that work out what they uniquely can give to the world, not just growth or money, but their excellence, their respect for others, or their ability to make people happy. Some call those things a soul," according to Charles Handy, an Irish author and philosopher who specializes in organizational behavior and management.[4]

"Soul. The word often sounds strange to modern ears. Terms like heart and soul seem almost exotic. We rarely think or talk about where we come from or what we are here to do. We need to. Otherwise, we deaden our souls, stunt our spirits, and live our lives halfheartedly."[5]

Soul is bigger than corporate culture because it is allied to the heart as well as the head and described by such abstractions as belonging, imagination, inspiration, commitment, attachment, and passion. People search for virtue and goodness in work and life: a meaningfulness that quenches their thirst for a sense of efficacy and purpose.

When soul is used in connection with schools, different visions surface. Soul moves beyond norms, myths, or standards; it focuses on spirit, possibilities, dreams, and ideals. It is not as rational as defining interaction patterns or organizational processes. Quantitative assessments are inadequate in measuring soul; it can only be experienced and felt.

Soul connects the heart with the mind and the spirit with work. Schools with a sense of their own soul have a feeling of connectedness and oneness with their mission, essence, and destiny. They are true to themselves and have a rich experience that endures in the memory and touches the heart. From the soul come feelings of rewarding work and fulfilling relationships. There is a depth of purpose and substance in these feelings.

Though most organizations covet conformity, the soul celebrates the individuality and variety in people and their personalities. For children, this means that they should be comfortable with themselves, without feeling as if they should lead a life reaching for the brass ring of material success established by others. Children cannot be something they are not, even to gratify parents or teachers or to achieve the goals established by others. The soul is about being and feeling, not just performing and conforming to fit into a mold someone else establishes.

Schools with soul are sanctuaries for children. The spirit and zeal in these schools creates an inner strength for adults and children. Failure is not mourned. After all, life's lessons come wrapped in different and unexpected packages. Wisdom does not fly in on gossamer wings and warm breezes: it is sometimes discovered in the dark places of disappointment and even sadness.

The soul is where creativity, imagination, and adaptability reside, and from this comes commitment and innovation. Warmth and humanness is never lost in work that is joyful and rewarding. In these environments, children feel a sense of curiosity and involvement in work that nourishes and rekindles the spirit.

Schools that lack spirit fail to reach exceptional levels of performance. The spirit develops an aura that inspires and prods people's thoughts and behavior and propels them to new heights and to overcome the odds. Although intelligent outcomes are necessary, all schools with goodness and virtue have a definable spirit that cannot be legislated or mandated. From spirit, great commitment and achievements flow.

Old theories of leadership emphasized the intellect but leadership has a spiritual dimension, too. Soulful leadership is about keeping the moral imperative around what the schools are to be and about building long-lasting bonds between people. Leadership brings people together to pursue meaning and to rekindle passion and purpose: it is not about acting as the hero who rides into the breach to save the day.

Leadership connects the head and heart around the idea and values of a place called school. Weathering hardships and defeats and taking on new challenges are part of their obligation. Leaders have a sense of calling and empathy for people and unbounded optimism and unwavering adherence to principles.

SOUL, GOODNESS, AND INTEGRITY

The integrity of schools is centered on idealism and values. Integrity is where soul and practice overlap—where abstract values, ideals, and principles converge with clear purpose and consistent practice. The congruence between performance and ideals is testament to its integrity or lack thereof.

A school's soul is defined by moral standards, ethics, and goodness. All are interlinked and interdependent. They each raise a set of issues, which, if addressed and pursued, leads to greater integrity. The practice of the school, its curricular, instructional, and assessment program, plus its operational policies and procedures, must fit tightly with the essence of its values and sense of goodness.

The basic concepts that can help a school live the essence of its soul include:

- Educators who discuss and assess whether their schools exhibit virtue, goodness, and values. They raise and discuss the philo-

sophical and moral questions about what schools are and what they should be.
- Intangible spirit and energy, beliefs and assumptions, as well as values, ethics, and principles compose organizational "soul."
- Schools that commit to justice, equality, and truth have greater virtue than those geared to management and processes.
- Justice, equality, and truth must be at the essence of the relationships in schools with "soul."

Meaning in life comes from having purpose. School must provide the environment where a sense of goodness exists and where both children and teachers gain greater insight into themselves. In these schools, there is peace with oneself, a feeling of forgiveness for others, and a sense of wonder and poetry about life. Human caring and a compassionate community are created.

SCHOOLS AS SANCTUARIES

Children are not products or human capital. Children are simply children who need a place to grow and develop safely and happily.

Children need the sanctity to be themselves, to learn and mature, and to take risks so that they can garner the experience of life without paying devastating consequences. In these "sanctuaries" human genius in all its forms is honored and fostered.[6]

Children need safe havens and the safety and solace to be who they are and to escape the trials and tribulations of daily life and difficulties at home and in their neighborhoods. They find respite from external pressures and heal from the unpredictability of life. Children come with a variety of personalities, abilities, and philosophies, and they all must find acceptance and understanding. Life can be hectic for children as they travel the path from childhood to maturity and face all the social, economic, and personal issues that adults confront.

A passionate spirit, strong emotional bonds, and intellectual challenge exemplify schools as sanctuaries. The qualities such schools share are:

- Sense of Wonder—The wonder of curiosity, imagination, and creativity are not secondary priorities, because no matter the age, these characteristics motivate and stimulate people. Children are spontaneous and explore and ask questions or make comments that spur more thought and reflection. The expressiveness of childhood is not lost, and innocence is the catalyst that produces the magic of learning in its purist form.
- Reverence—Wisdom is revered and children learn that both the head and the heart are important. Wisdom, which is far more than mastery of content, requires an understanding of principles and values, coupled with a sense of the common good beyond self-interest. Regardless of their abilities or station in life, children must honor their responsibilities and obligations with the guidance and affectionate prodding of teachers and mentors. Education liberates the mind and the spirit and helps students to break self-imposed limitations and boundaries. The inestimable potential of children's lives is aroused and supported.
- Passion—Schools are not places of ambivalence and neutrality. They abound with passion, just like the children within them. Educating children evokes deep feelings of excitement and efficacy where passion is transformed into commitment. The moral imperative to help children invigorates the passion to build places for children that are inspired and joyful. Passion, coupled with perseverance, gives birth to the power of imagination.
- Connectedness—In these schools, children belong and are connected to the people within the school, and they see connections to the outside world. As sanctuaries, schools are clear about their values and ideals; they build strong bonds with children and their families. Children learn that their behavior and attitude have an impact on themselves and others and can be a constructive or destructive force socially, ethically, and individually. They begin to see themselves as competent—not deficient or defective—individuals.
- Purpose—In these schools, everyone is a learner: children and adults. They share the excitement of learning something new and of struggling with mastering innovative things. The curricula reflect strong academic understandings in all the disciplines, including the fine arts. The intellect is appreciated, and matters of the

heart are celebrated. Character is cultivated as well as knowledge and skills.
- Idealism—Strong ideals exemplify these schools because ideals are lofty and noble. People must stretch to reach them and not settle for pedestrian goals of basic literacy or application of skills. Sanctuaries pursue virtue, democratic values, and knowledge so that students gain the wisdom to act on them. Knowledge and content change with research and time, but these concepts provide the ballast and compass for adjusting to new times and complex issues.
- Safety—Children have a right to feel safe physically, emotionally, and intellectually. Safety of the mind and spirit as well as the body needs to be a part of every school. Children need protection from verbal assaults, emotional muggings, and intellectual attacks. They need the warmth of compassion to express feelings and emotions, the security to express ideas no matter how divergent or imaginative, and the assurance that they do not have to worry about their physical safety.

In safe schools, there are no haves and have-nots or "chosen ones" and outcasts. There is no standardized mold in which all children must fit. Children are safe to be who they are as products of their heritage, parents, potential, and experience.

We must be loyal to the wonder of childhood in all its stages. To do so takes courage because open discussion of schools as sanctuaries brings scoffing and charges of näiveté from those whose perceptions are stuck in the quicksand of engineering and pragmatism. To be an idealist takes fortitude to champion the cause of educating children in matters of the intellect and the heart.

Courage is a matter of heart. Pushing against the grain, standing up for principles, and holding one's own against peers, conventional wisdom, and "the way we always do things" takes strength of character.

Schools are not about organizational structures, power, procedures, or management. They are about the promise of living. They are about relationships and interactions that form the nucleus around which learning and growth occur. Children become educated through the energy created from a deep connection with teachers, peers, and others. Viewing schools as impersonal, metrically driven organizations falls short of what they really mean in a person's life.

Schools ought to be places where people have their heads in the clouds. In these sanctuaries, human genius in all its forms is honored, and the efforts of children who persevere with intensity, drive, and integrity of purpose are applauded.

ESSENTIAL IDEAS TO REMEMBER

- Schools are not like corporations that push for profit. Schools have a sense of soul that fosters care and love for children and work to help them to develop their abilities and to find success and happiness in life.
- Leadership is about love—working with teachers and others so that they may fulfill themselves at work and in their life's purpose.
- The school's integrity rests on a sense of goodness and a commitment to justice, equality, and the search for truth.
- Schools are sanctuaries for children so that they may be themselves, take risks, and learn and grow.

NOTES

1. William J. O'Brien, *Character at Work* (New York: Paulist Press, 2008), 3.
2. Mihaly Csikszentmihalyi, *Good Business* (New York: Viking, 2003), 145.
3. O'Brien, *Character at Work*, 105.
4. Charles Handy, www.brainyquote.com/quotes/quotes/c/charleshan130761.html#y0ZiSPgexU0CjuUl.99.
5. Lee G. Bolman and Terrence E. Deal, *Leading with Soul* (San Francisco: Jossey-Bass, 1995), 2.
6. George A. Goens, *Soft Leadership for Hard Times* (Lanham, MD: Rowman & Littlefield, 2005), 137–41.

Part III

What We Must Do

10

MORAL IMPERATIVE

> All human beings tend to have moral senses, which is the categorical imperative for them to act.—Immanuel Kant

Schools are supposed to be "good" places, not pressure cookers. Goodness has to do with virtue, a word rarely used when describing or discussing schools. Along with ethics, virtue has been buried and isn't referenced in many discussions on reform. Shouldn't virtue be a primary focus when dealing with children?

Education should be a virtuous process, and schools should be paragons of principled goals and ethics. Virtue in education means conforming to a standard of right, which carries with it a moral dimension and also relates to efficacy. Education is empowering and carries with it efficacy and strength. Right action and thinking based on values and standards are prerequisites for professional practice.

Virtuous schools teach children to question, challenge, and seek answers. Intellectual curiosity is seen as a strength, not a nuisance. Mistakes are perceived as opportunities, not as failures. Teachers help children to understand that their fulfillment and happiness depend, in part, on the full use of their intellectual capacities and enthusiasm and drive.

Historically, public schools had the moral imperative to educate children. They served children but were also a positive unifying institution for communities, tied to the community's identity and a source of pride. They exemplified the American dream.

Because of public education's moral imperative, we must question the thinking behind practices and reforms. We must challenge special interest perspectives, programs, profit, and propaganda. Today, reforms focus on markets with emphasis on competition both internally within the schools and externally with competitors. Education is too important to be diminished through simplistic platitudes and special interests.

Teaching is a moral and ethical undertaking that involves providing a standard of care for children of all ages and backgrounds and being held responsible for doing so. Ethics are essential because they involve questions of right and wrong, duties and obligations, and rights and responsibilities.

Teachers are responsible for raising questions and fulfilling the moral imperative for schools to be true to the principles of justice, fairness, liberty, honesty, respect, dignity, and truth. The integrity and credibility of schools depend on whether and how they meet these principles.

Decisions must be based on the needs of all children, not on special interests, profit margins, or publicity. Reforms must be focused on children's needs. Technology is not promoted at the expense of teacher-student relationships, testing at the expense of higher order thinking, or short-term goals at the expense of educating children to nurture their talents and abilities. Schools are transparent and approachable, not closed and focused on profit, political, or social agendas.

Many reformers today look at schools as technical or business enterprises that simply require procedures and measurable accountability to be successful. Most of these rational reforms have narrowed the corridor of local decision making, narrowed the curriculum, and narrowed learning to rote regurgitation. Education is more than that, and the role of teachers is more complicated than following a routine or designated methods. Human connection is essential in order to apply techniques and approaches successfully.

Our moral obligation is to prepare children to participate effectively in social and civic life, as well as to develop and pursue their talents and interests. Educators' moral obligations to all children include:

a. Preparing children to participate in our political and social democracy and to understand our constitutional system and representative government. Children must understand their obligations in fulfilling the principles of freedom, liberty, justice, equality, and fairness, as well as comprehend the balance of individual rights and the common good.

b. Providing mastery of communication, economic, scientific, cultural, and fine arts subject matter, as well as the reasoning skills of analysis, synthesis, and evaluation.
c. Exposing children to quality instruction and teaching that involve both the art and science of pedagogy. Creativity in classrooms stimulates curiosity and interest.
d. Serving as stewards of the school, its mission, and purpose through creating, questioning, and living espoused values and sustaining a culture of change and improvement.
e. Helping children to look inside themselves and define their ambitions and motivation, discover how they connect with the larger world, and pursue purpose and meaning.

Responsibilities and obligations are not necessarily synonymous. Responsibilities define the extent of authority and activities often specified in job descriptions and the like. They are frequently the result of statutes, organizational documents, or master contracts. Meeting role responsibilities does not necessarily mean meeting obligations.

Obligations, on the other hand, come from a different source. They define our sense of duty that must be met for moral or legal reasons. Obligation, conscience, and duty are powerful forces to do the right thing with a foundation in principles and ethical conduct.

Ethical obligations structure decisions and behavior for individual teachers and for the school community as a whole. The integrity, honor, and trustworthiness of schools rest on meeting obligations. Teachers have a duty to do what is good for children, not just what is expedient or mandated. They have ethical obligations, not just professional responsibilities.

The moral imperative of teachers is evident in both official and hidden curricula. Judgments about children cannot be based on irrelevant grounds like gender, race, or socioeconomic status. Teachers do not define children's destinies: each child must do that for him- or herself with the guidance and understanding of teachers. Teachers need to be sure that the values of justice and respect are accorded all children.

Children need to be protected from injustice. Schools that are just and fair

- shield people from discrimination on immaterial grounds;
- protect powerless people from exploitation or hurt through overt actions or indifference;
- provide equal opportunity to all;
- grant a voice for all children so that they can be a valued part of the larger school community;
- allow children the opportunity to try their wings and participate in events and activities without artificial judgments or culling;
- preserve the dignity of children;
- ensure children's freedom and liberty to be themselves and to participate democratically; and
- demonstrate integrity so that words and actions match positive values.

Minimally, the moral obligation of teachers is to do no harm, which is the fundamental precept of a code of ethics. In essence, teachers are advocates for children as they confront the official and the hidden curricula. If they are not advocates, who will be?

Teachers must protect children from the negative forces within the school's operation and from the official or the hidden curricula. Teachers with courage find the fortitude to help children and to mirror the spirit and soul of the school through ethical practice.

STRUCTURE AND ETHICS

Leading a school is a complex challenge complete with frustration and ambiguity because problems are not always clear and the causes may be out of the direct reach of the school. Solutions to the issues are beyond simplistic notions. Complications are omnipresent. Unintended consequences arise. All decisions are placed under the microscope of public scrutiny.

What structures decisions and efforts at change in organization? The question is: what is structure? When we think of restructuring, we usually think of roles, planning, organizing, coordinating, monitoring, and evaluating—and that's part of the problem.

Restructuring efforts are generally concerned with process—how decisions get made and implemented—top down, bottom up, or both ends toward the middle. Power and authority are the focus. Efficient and effective processes, as history demonstrates, may not always be ethical or moral.

We think of structure as hierarchical command-and-control and line-and-staff relationships. Carrots and sticks—rewards and punishment—become the way to direct and control behavior to be competitive.

Structure, however, is more than methods of organization or procedures to control people. We miss an important structure because we don't think of it as a structure. We don't consider ethics when we think of what shapes our personal and professional lives.

Ethics are powerful. Think about it. What "structures" our personal decisions? Most likely, the values, beliefs, norms, standards, and ethics we learned at home from our parents, in school, or at church. Ethics are far more potent than the monitoring and controlling mechanisms that organizations put in place to make sure that people behave properly. And they do not require additional staff—just a moral and ethical commitment.

Ethics are the cornerstones of any profession because they guide decisions and conduct in complex and difficult issues. In reality, they are an invisible force that leads and directs approaches and actions. They are more potent than traditional hierarchical power and controls because commitment to values and ethics are the glue of professional conduct.

Ethics concern professional standards of behavior, the guiding principles that govern professional conduct, and the exercise of judgment in the performance of their role. Because of the autonomy and specialized knowledge that professionals have, ethics are essential in determining right and wrong actions.

A commitment to professional standards far surpasses organizational controls, rewards or punishments, or administrative directives. Professionals internalize ethics and make them a part of their behavior because of their desire to perform to the highest conduct and their dedication to their oath and profession.

When chaos erupts, values provide the foundation for making "good" decisions and choices. People have confidence in leaders when decisions and actions are congruent with values. Commitment to standards builds a sense of community because values create meaning, and meaning motivates. In times of crisis these values provide equilibrium and stability.

Confusing and perplexing times propel people to seek answers to make sense of the world around them. Difficult issues, conflicting demands, and controversy engulf us and can be overwhelming. A code of ethics guides teachers when confronted by these ambiguous, bewildering issues that ache for resolution, particularly when the alternatives are difficult, unclear, or explosive.

Ideals and principles provide guidance to do what is "right." They create positive conflict, raise issues, and require dialogue and contemplation, which produce clarity of purpose and truthful thought and action. Ethics are those anchor points around which we frame responses and decisions in our professional lives to do what is right. They are also the foundation upon which people stand when things go awry, compromising professional and personal standards.

All of this translates into the following operational values: to help children learn, the school itself must be a learning community. This community must believe that every student can learn, and it does everything in its power to ensure that it happens. This community provides for the child's academic, developmental, physical, and social needs through professional commitment. Respect is evident throughout the community for children, teachers, support staff, administrators, and parents, as well as the greater community. The learning community is a partnership of reciprocal rights and obligations among parents, teachers, and others.

In essence, schools should be unyielding in regard to values and ethics and flexible regarding procedures to creatively find solutions to the challenges of educating students and opening their minds and hearts. Leadership involves values that connect people around a common purpose. Without strong organizational values, schools can drift, resulting in a Machiavellian drive where the ends justify the means. When times are difficult, some leaders push their organizations into behavior contrary to their stated values and mission.

Values are more than motherhood, country, and apple pie. They define behavior that is in harmony with these values and guide the school's internal conduct and relationships with parents, students, colleges, and community. In fact, part of evaluating employee performance should be based on whether or not they adhere to the values and beliefs of the school and profession.

Values create an organization's identity—what it stands for, what it is, and what it wants to be.[1] People do not work for only cash or profit; they want meaningful work and a foundation for positive relationships.

POSITIVE CONFLICT

Organizational values "evoke positive emotion, stimulate creativity, and propel self-regulation or peer regulation."[2] They also raise issues and conflict. Teachers may challenge their principal or superintendent about whether certain approaches of a program violate the school district's values. Strong value statements will do that. Parents may also raise issues about whether the schools do what they say they are going to do.

Discussion and debate about integrity to an organization's values are very constructive. Values can be interpreted in several ways, and having that conversation is important for a deeper understanding of their meaning and implementation. Important issues may be raised, which otherwise might have been overlooked.

Healthy conflict raises the kind of discord that produces thought and reflection. People challenge whether the operations and programs have integrity to the espoused values and principles. Without integrity, credibility is lost and the organization is morally bankrupt.

Conflict can build bridges, create greater understanding, and offer the sense of greater efficacy when people listen. These discussions build commitment; they don't destroy it. Constructive dialogue clarifies collective and individual thought and provides for the development of shared understanding and commitment, which leads to problem solving.

Value-based leadership and relationships are absolutely essential. Those drenched in the intoxication of hierarchical power ultimately destroy a value-oriented organization and curtail any dialogue or creative and innovative approaches to meeting the organization's challenges. Leaders can destroy the integrity of the organization as well as their own trustworthiness.

Credibility builds support and respect, which is essential from students, parents, and the community. It's not really all that complicated. Strong principles are the building blocks upon which quality organizations for schools are developed. Without them, organizations float on the sea of expediency and eventually drown through the weight of the corruption of their values.

The current reform movement's focus is on metric-based accountability processes. Outside of a few platitudes, these approaches do not examine the importance of values to teachers and other professionals. They look for short-term metrical progress sometimes at the expense of high-mindedness.

Teachers are obligated to meet a professional "standard of care" in working with children. All teachers must adhere to this ethical standard. Physicians of all types—from surgeons to psychiatrists—must meet a standard of care with their patients because they work on the physical, psychological, or social dispositions of their clients. So do teachers, but to a different degree.

When working in such a complex environment, values and ethics define principled behavior that children and parents deserve. Holding tight around those values and ethics allows creative, appropriate, and innovative paths and solutions to be found. They establish the groundwork for thinking and problem solving.

THINKING AND PROBLEM SOLVING

Conceptual thinkers see the world in multifaceted ways. They often see shades of gray, and they can live with ambiguity and uncertainty because they do not expect the world to be an orderly and tidy place composed of black and white questions.

Consequently, confusion is tolerable because change occurs with disequilibrium and its resulting residue of unanticipated outcomes. Disconfirming data and information are a consequence of disequilibrium and some resulting chaos. Leaders adjust their thinking and possibly disregard past practice. They transform, help others to transform, and transform organizations and society through ideas and principles.

Physicist David Bohm asserts that there is a potential problem with thinking—fragmentation—which breaks our world into discrete bits and pieces.³ This approach to thinking is not holistic; it's silo thinking. Organizations are based on this mind-set. Breaking our world into isolated pieces creates phalanxes of specialists and a concoction of silos. Socially, we divide ourselves as a nation into groups of hyphenated citizens. We try to bring about change in each silo, as if it is totally separate and discrete rather than a component of a larger unit, then we get frustrated as problems continue to erupt and nothing changes.

The scientific method emphasizes analysis: carving a problem or issue into parts and components and addressing each part, which is a fragmented approach. Holistic thought, however, examines complete entities and the forceful and subtle dynamics that affect conditions and the web of interconnections and relationships. Systems thinking considers organizations as interconnected, dynamic, and evolving integral entities. The integral nature of things and their subtle interconnections have great consequences.

Our thoughts are not isolated from how we perceive our total being. Through fragmented thinking, we see our mind as where thought resides, our body as where our physical being is housed, and our emotions as where our feelings are contained. But we are not that distinct. Our thoughts affect our feelings and can create physical conditions and symptoms and vice versa. Our physical health affects our emotions and thinking. We are a whole being integrally connected through head, heart, and spirit—all interwoven and inseparable. We are not just a conglomeration of independent parts.

How we think is important because it permeates everything we do and how we do it. In essence, thought creates our world and our own reality: it is not simply benign or philosophical pondering, because we act on thought.

Trying to remain aware of the whole is difficult because traditionally we have been trained in part-to-whole management approaches. Fragmented thinking is evident in our organizations with their emphasis on structure and departments, functions and responsibilities, and roles and responsibilities. Knowledge is disjointed and can become distorted and dangerous because parts may not be characteristic of the whole. What may be appropriate for one part may be hazardous to the others. With some reformers, the single fragment approach—quantitative metrics—can weaken and destroy the purpose of the entire institution.

In schools today we focus on structures and standards and the continual metrical analysis of the parts. By collecting data on skills and concepts, we think we will understand the health of the whole. We study variables as if they were separate and distinct, trying to identify the ones that will cause the others to react in positive ways.

As Margaret Wheatley indicated, power is generated by relationships. Our relationships are more important than how functions and tasks are organized. The energy from positive relationships is the power that produces creativity, because people are really "bundles of potential" that, if capitalized, can change the world. "We need leaders to understand that we are best controlled by concepts that invite our participation, not policies and procedures that curtail our contribution."[4] This is a far cry from the competitive and divisive approaches of school reform wherein teachers are painted as inept, self-interested union mongers who need to be regulated.

Shaking people's perceptions and thinking about their world in new ways is important. Ideas capture the imagination, stir creativity, and excite the spirit, all activities of the soul. The power of ideas is fundamental to efforts of changing and producing schools with a sense of goodness.

Ideas, particularly noble and important ones, form fields of thought, which generate energy and motivation, and establish new structures and processes. Unfortunately, ideas are viewed as esoteric or philosophical and are not always seen or understood as a catalyst for change. What is more pragmatic, however, than an idea?

Ideas and the force fields around them help people to see the integral nature of concepts because they produce power and dialogue. Ideas help people to make sense of the uncertainty and ambiguity with which they struggle. Concepts provide a framework for us to understand the confusion—or at least to assist us in thinking about it in a productive way without being immobilized.

Values and ethics provide a gauge to determine good practice and relationships relating to a positive standard of care for children. What happens when schools fall off the track? What can leaders and others really do? School reform and other initiatives seem immune to accountability as the media and political parade continues. Politics and corporatization are powerful.

ETHICS AND OUTRAGE

So what does this all mean for school leaders and educators? Quite simply, there are times that they must lead by outrage. No, not running around with their hair on fire, using brute coercion or emulating hockey enforcers. It's deeper than that.

Leadership by outrage is a symbolic act that highlights what is principled and right when proposals, policies, and practices are detrimental to children and to the institution of public education. Speaking out and standing up for values and principles and acting on convictions takes moral courage.

A case in point is teacher accountability and evaluation. So-called reformers and special interests propose assessing teachers using student achievement tests, value added or otherwise.

The question here is one of ethics and proper practice. Should schools implement a process of teacher accountability that is disparaged through research, that is insensitive to the conditions beyond teachers' control, that is vacuous of the psychometric issues of reliability and validity, and that is indifferent to the effects of poverty, family conditions, nutrition, parent support, community safety, and other factors?

Teachers have a right to be evaluated through ethical assessment systems. Standing against these proposals is not without risk because the media and some political interests have advocated testing as a simple solution to a complex and complicated circumstance. Political expedience can collide with ethical and professional practice. Taking a stand and educating board members, the community, and politicians is difficult because of simplistic media stories, heavily funded advocates, and political power groups. Some special interest groups have economic, political, or personal stakes in these proposals.

If educators don't speak out, who will? They must lead and stand on professional ideals and ethical standards. They must not simply maintain and supervise systems. They must develop programs based on a standard of care for children, support teachers and their development, and build confidence and credibility within the community. They must move beyond short-term metrics and focus on the long term based on the welfare of children and the institution of public education. They must challenge politicians, celebrities, and special interests in defense of education and the common good.

Acting on principle and ethics is at the heart of leadership. Public education needs leaders who stand up for the underlying vision and values of education in our democratic society and culture. They must be committed to the purpose of public education, its history, security, and underlying values and commitments to children. The principles of justice, equality, liberty, goodness, truth, and beauty have been and should remain at the core of public education for all children.

Professionalism carries with it an ethical imperative to stand up for one's principles and to speak the truth to power. Educators must not kowtow on the basis of politics, finances, or political favor when the education and care of children are endangered or compromised. There are political and professional hazards to leading with integrity. But standing silent when reform proposals are destructive to public education is not honorable leadership.

Former senator Bill Bradley stated that leaders "should change us to think anew, remind us of the goodness that lies within each of us, and inspire us with the courage they demonstrate by telling us the truth."[5] The late Tom Sergiovanni indicated that leaders have a duty to "lead by outrage" when things are amiss.[6] James MacGregor Burns, in his seminal book *Leadership*, states that leaders "do not shun conflict; they confront it, exploit it, and ultimately embody it."[7] People unite around the values of justice, equality, and human dignity.

Leaders must do what is right. Speak out and stand up for what is ethically correct to provide a well-researched professional standard of care and programs for our children. To remain silent or to take financial carrots and move ahead with professionally or ethically questionable proposals destroys the credibility of educational leaders and eventually shatters the ideals of public education.

We must stand on and for professional values, ethical practice, and quality research so that our children have the care and opportunity to learn and grow and meet their potential.

ESSENTIAL IDEAS TO REMEMBER

- Schools and teachers have a moral imperative to create schools of goodness where children can grow, learn, and develop.

- Teachers and all educators have a moral responsibility to take actions and to make decisions that are based on professional ethics and values.
- Ethics and values are structures that define the nature, mission, decisions, and behavior of teachers and other educators.
- How we think determines how we define issues, make decisions, and pursue actions in problem solving.
- There are times when educators must lead by outrage.

NOTES

1. Margaret Wheatley, *Finding our Way: Leadership in Uncertain Times* (San Francisco: Berrett-Koehler, 2005), 118–19.

2. Rosabeth Moss Kantor, "How Great Companies Think Differently," *Harvard Business Review*, November 2011.

3. David Bohm, *Thought As a System* (New York: Routledge, 1994).

4. Margaret Wheatley, *Leadership and the New Science* (San Francisco: Berrett-Koehler, 2006), 131.

5. Bill Bradley, *We Can All Do Better* (New York: Vanguard Press, 2012), 160.

6. Thomas Sergiovanni, *Value-Added Leadership* (New York: Harcourt, Brace, Jovanovich, 1990), 134.

7. James MacGregor Burns, *Leadership* (New York: Harper Torchbooks, 1978), 39.

11

WHAT WE MUST DO

The ultimate test of a moral society is the kind of world that it leaves to its children.—Dietrich Bonhoeffer

A fog of reform has clouded our vision and scope. Things have become confused, complex, and complicated as we try to quantify everything with simplistic measures.

Instruments and technology cannot forecast our organizational and social "weather" with certainty, and they certainly cannot foretell how people will relate and interact in the complex web of human relationships. Unanticipated consequences sprout without warning. The certainty and control are lost in the confluence of people's lives and relationships. Force fields composed of the emotional, creative, and intellectual energy of human beings and the heart, imagination, and beliefs they bring with them are immune to technological analysis. Quantitative analysis cannot determine the potential or value of people.

The windstorm of criticism of public education has been withering. The problem is that amid the cacophony of criticism the truth is fogged behind well-financed special interest campaigns and dubious research or selective interpretation of research. In addition, complicated legislation like No Child Left Behind and Race to the Top emphasizes test scores and metrical targets. No wonder the truth is buried or obscured.

Myths circulate in the media about some reforms. Charter schools are given mythical status even though traditional public schools "typically outperform charter schools" when like groups are compared; in addition, the media "play down the impact of charter school failures."[1]

Cyber schools are another overstated reform. Cyber schooling is big business, but the results are dismal. Dropout rates often exceed 50 percent and graduation rates are "abysmal." Students enrolled in the "Tennessee Virtual Academy—operated by K–12 Inc., scored lower than any of the other 1,300 elementary schools on the state's standardized test."[2]

In addition, we must be wary of the influence of the educational-industrial complex. The movement to privatize education and redirect monies from public schools to vouchers, charters, educational management organizations, and publishers of testing materials must be challenged. The research, slogans, and marketing by the educational-industrial complex must be contested.

Our nation needs to return to a sense of soul—to a place where spirit and values matter. We need wisdom, not metrics. We need truth, not politically correct garble. We need to believe in the common good, not special interests. We need credibility and courageous actions, not pandering and political hype. We need courageous action and authentic leadership, not Madison Avenue brands, celebrity, and slogans.

How we get there begins with honest dialogue and renewing our values and principles. We must move beyond the belief that technology will save us to the knowledge that only we can save ourselves. We must reignite skepticism and straight talk. We must take our civic responsibility seriously and speak out.

When all is said and done, schools are really about the promise of living: the promise that our sons or daughters can have fulfilling lives. That's why education is so important: it's not only about immediate or superficial test results, but also the long-term journey our children take in life and the quality of their relationships, intellect, and emotional contentment.

We have to rethink reforms and rethink schools. Most parents understand that their children learn with their hearts as well as their heads, physically as well as intellectually, and intuitively as well as linearly. Imagination—as well as logic—is important. As we watch our children grow, greater emphasis must be placed on imaginative and creative thinking than on rote responses.

Creativity is essential. "Education is not a linear process of preparation for the future. It is about cultivating the talents and sensibilities through which we can live our best lives in the present and create a future for ourselves."[3] Creativity, imagination, joy, ingenuity, and wonder are the foundation for a well-educated and civil society. They must not be extinguished from our schools. The foundation for the success of our children, our country, and the common good is found in strong values.

Frequently when we look at children, our expectations for them are based on their chronological age. That seems awfully simplistic, because their intellectual, physical, or emotional ages may not be reflected in their chronological age. Some are more mature than others and have deeper insights than their peers. Others require more time. Parents, educators, and society in general lack patience in terms of the impact of education on children. Meeting one's full potential takes time—after all, becoming fully educated is a lifelong voyage.

In today's classroom, we expect all teachers to make "adequate yearly progress" with all children based on test score analysis. Yet these same children come to school with some of the issues that psychologists and psychiatrists indicate are debilitating for adults in their work and personal lives. We don't expect those who may be going through severe family crises, death, or divorce to perform at the same levels that they did prior to their personal crises. Many employers provide a safety net for employees so that they can return to past levels of productivity. These conditions can compromise test scores and analytic projections for children.

Parents and educators can do several things to create sanctuaries where kids can grow and develop. First, we must jettison our fear of failure. Scientists fail consistently as they try to find breakthroughs. But our school's progress is hindered because of a four-letter word: fear. It destroys creativity and drive. Competitive statistics shackle effort and risk taking. Children's self-concept is shattered because of the expectation for perfection and winning.

Some parents don't want their children to struggle. Children themselves want to avoid it. But there are lessons to be learned when children are given the space to struggle and problem solve. When they do, confidence builds and they gain self-assurance in their own abilities. Self-esteem grows organically, not through false praise or gimmicks. In addition, they will not fear failure, but understand that in it there are messages and passages to success.

To paraphrase Proust, we must see with new eyes. Take a deep look at what is and what could be. We cannot be constrained by the talking heads and corporate individuals who have other motives beyond the common good. We have to understand that top-down control from Washington will not really improve the relationships that exist between children and their teachers in local schools. Parents working with teachers and local school board members have much more direct control over what happens to their children than if that control came from corporations, the state capital, or congress and the president.

We must all work to improve the conditions of children, including their health, classroom conditions, and family life. We must continually look through the eyes of a child, maintaining a sense of innocence, a feeling of joy, and a sense of excitement about learning. Schools must capitalize on the innocence of children and support their joy in learning, their curiosity, their spontaneity, and their imagination. They should not be places of stressful drudgery.

For our children to live a life of happiness, we must help them on several fronts. An important aspect of education is helping children to find their calling in life. Within us there's a driving force that calls to us to do certain things with the time we have on the planet. The beauty of it is that it's different for each individual. One person's calling very well may be tedium for another person. That's the beauty of life and our uniqueness.

Second, we must help our children define the positive principles and values that lead to a life of wisdom. We don't all have to be philosophers. But we all have to live life on positive principles and ethics so that we make wise decisions that are good for us as individuals, that are good for others, and that are good for the commonweal.

We need to help children understand that they are responsible for their lives and actions. They are not victims. Teaching victimhood rots their potential and talent, because they think that they are helpless and impotent to respond to life's challenges or to other people's opinions or expectations. Life isn't always easy, but our children have to know that even in the most difficult of times, they can respond in a way that is based on positive values and principles and they can reach for virtue. To be empowered, children first need a sense of their own efficacy.

Children have to understand that the world is a place of disequilibrium, chaos, and irrationality, but is also playful, serendipitous, and self-renewing. Principles and values help us all to get through the chaos of life. Those principles and values also help us to lead a life of integrity. Inevitably at some point in children's lives, they will face very difficult choices or losses. One way to survive and learn from those times is by understanding that they can respond based on principle.

Finally, we must teach children to recognize that strong connections and relationships between people are necessary for creativity, productivity, and commitment. Relationships should not be constrained by walls, shields, or defenses constructed by one's own self-concept, nor by others. Common purpose and creativity are the result of positive relationships where people can take the true risk to be their real selves. Children will not reach their potential if they are aloof loners or above the fray. It's not how much you know, but about the integrity, honesty, and genuineness with which you address issues and life.

In essence, we must understand that ideas, feelings, and passion are all part of our humanity. Our job is to help our students live wholeheartedly and become visible to the world and contribute their gifts and talents—the very heart of their being—to humanity. That's what schools help them do. That's the conversation we must have if our children's futures are to be open and bright.

HAPPY LIVES

We all want children to live "happy" lives. What does that mean, really? Such an abstraction can mean everything, yet nothing at all. It's a generalization that at one time or another parents state as an aspiration for their children. And schools are supposed to be the highways to happiness.

An education provides some of the tools that help people pursue happiness, but getting degrees or doing well academically does not necessarily guarantee it. Plenty of people in this country have prestigious degrees tacked to their walls but live lives of quiet desperation.

We all want children to find happiness. To some, it means having "things" and all of one's wants met. Meeting all of our "wants" does not bring happiness. In fact, wants can create conflict within our own spirit and with others and their so-called wants. Simply accumulating the things we want does not lead to a good life.

A life of happiness, according to philosopher Mortimer Adler, has a moral dimension. He makes a distinction between needs and wants: "by needs, I mean those desires which are inherent in human nature in which, therefore, are the same for all human beings everywhere and at all times. By wants, I mean those desires which arise in individuals as a result of the particular circumstances of their lives."[4]

Needs, he argues, are right desires. We all need liberty, justice, respect, and dignity. The government can work to ensure that all of us have these needs met. Government, however, cannot secure our wants for us.

Aristotle said that a good life is one that is lived in "accordance with moral virtue."[5] Individuals lead good and happy lives if they live them ethically and with honor. No one can make another's life happy. Each individual must make the moral and ethical decisions to do so, and that's a lifelong proposition.

Parents and teachers have a unique responsibility to create a place—home and school—where children can grow and follow their destiny. Creativity, curiosity, and passion are part of the educational process. However, because of reform today, those characteristics seem lost in rote recitation, avatar-driven computer programs, and a curriculum limited to basic skills. Something is seriously wrong when we focus more on tests and competition than on helping children to discover their passion and purpose in life.

Certainly to pursue happiness children require social and academic competence as well as personal confidence and commitment. Finding their passion is part of helping them to discover who they are so that they become self-aware and find what they truly love. In a sense, people make themselves visible to the world and devote themselves to creativity and competence in pursuing their calling. Happiness is the result of the pursuit.

No guarantees of happiness exist. The government can't make us happy, nor can anyone else. We must find it for ourselves, and so must our children. We have to be in harmony with ourselves to be truly happy. Harmony is a quality of nature. Looking within and determining what is in us—what drives us and what tickles our fancy—is important. Artificial attachments to material things, social position, and recognition from others do not result in happiness and fulfillment. However, passion and calling will.

A calling exists in all children that destiny beckons them to fulfill. When they do, they are in their "element" and find and commit to their passions. When children find their calling, they are willing to engage in practice and work and become devoted to it. Work has a sense of flow.

When we are doing things that we love that drive us, time moves at warp speed and we are in a state of "flow," as renowned psychologist Csikszentmihalyi said, "so the link between flow and happiness depends on whether the flow-producing activity is complex, whether it leads to new challenges and hence to personal as well as cultural growth."[6]

We have to be honest about our "dark side." We have weaknesses and imperfections, and we sometimes fall short of our values and principles. The dark side can produce guilt and shame, bind us to the past, and dampen the feeling that we deserve to be happy. Taking a realistic look at ourselves and forgiving ourselves and moving ahead on a principled and meaningful path is essential. We are all weak at times and we are all flawed in some way—that is being human.

Happiness also depends on how we handle what comes to us in life and how we interpret it. Some people always think the sky is falling, while others see opportunity and challenge in the unexpected and convoluted things that come down the pike. We don't always have to "make things happen": sometimes the answer lies in letting things emerge naturally by allowing ideas and dreams to unfold. Happiness often comes when we just let things go. Clinging to the past or pursuing ventures for the wrong reasons, like vanity or ego, is destructive. They stymie passion and stop emotional and spiritual growth.

Happiness and significance come from pursuing noble goals—reaching for those unattainable principles and values that are the basis for a life of wisdom. Sounds like a recipe for frustration, doesn't it? But it isn't. Working hard for something we love leads to an exciting life of merit and virtue: a life worth living.

People flourish if they find meaning in life, and meaning brings contentment. Happiness is found within ourselves and in the pursuit of becoming a complete human being—using our talents, meeting our potential, and finding wisdom. The pursuit brings fulfillment.

Sometimes, uncovering the truth within us liberates us to be free to follow our bliss. Being in a state of comfortable indifference to life is not rewarding. Passion, however, is a creative and vibrant space—energizing. Nothing good gets done without a person with the zeal to do what others say cannot be done: to respond with love in times of hate and to be open to the beauty of the world and not succumb to the plastic pitfalls of society.

Happiness is found in our relationships with others. We all yearn for a sense of belonging in life. The feeling of being connected, accepted, and valued. At times we need someone to lean on in times of joy or pain. That's built into our souls. We are not intended to live in isolation. Relationships require that we act with virtue and avoid harmful behavior toward others. Focusing on giving rather than receiving brings great rewards.

What this means is that we have to make a commitment to a way of being—a way of life. The commitment to acting in loving, compassionate, and caring ways produces a life of strong and happy relationships with others and, importantly, with ourselves. Altruism, not selfishness, is being in harmony with the nature of life. Happiness is found in the principle of goodness.

In the quest for goodness, we must lead a disciplined life of character. When we are not true to noble principles and don't live up to the best in us, our conscience lets us know we veered off course. In our hearts we know we can do better. Happiness comes from the good we can do.

Technology, metrics, and data cannot lead us to happiness. Vaclav Havel said it well: "we enjoy all the achievements of modern civilization that have made our physical existence easier in so many important ways. Yet we do not know exactly what to do with ourselves, where to turn. The world of our experiences seems chaotic, confusing. Experts can explain anything in the objective world to us, yet we understand our own lives less and less. We live in the post-modern world, where everything is possible and almost nothing is certain."[7]

ESSENTIAL IDEAS TO REMEMBER

- Helping children get an education opens them to finding their passion in life and living a happy life.
- Education is not a simple, linear process of facts and figures. Cultivating talent and creativity are goals that affect individuals for a lifetime.

- Children grow and learn in individual ways and on individual time lines. Standardized tests do not characterize individual's potential, future, or character.
- Happiness is not the fulfillment of "wants." Happiness comes from fulfilling needs in finding and pursuing our passion.

NOTES

1. David Berliner and Gene V. Glass, *50 Myths and Lies That Threaten America's Public Schools* (New York: Teacher's College Press, 2014), 22.

2. Berliner and Glass, *50 Myths and Lies*, 33.

3. Ken Robinson, *Out of Our Minds* (New York: Capstone Publishing, 2011), 245.

4. Mortimer Adler, *Reforming Education: Opening of the American Mind* (New York: Collier Books, 1997), 84.

5. Adler, *Reforming Education*, 85.

6. Mihalyi Csikszentmihalyi, *Creativity* (New York: HarperCollins, 1996), 124.

7. Vaclav Havel, "The New Measure of Man," *New York Times*, July 8, 1994, A15.

12

THE FOG OF REFORM

Lessons

Be prepared to re-examine your reasoning.—Robert McNamara

The plans you make are too small for you to live.—David Whyte

Schools are places of hope and optimism. Children come to them with aspirations and passion. Public schools are about the common good and helping children reach their full potential and pursue their dreams.

Schools are not businesses geared to profit, ego, or special interest agendas. They are simply designed for children, where challenges exist, creativity thrives, and progress endures.

Education is more than mastery of skills. Learning values—respect, civility, open-mindedness, persistence, compassion, self-discipline—is important because we live in a democracy and social context. Historically, public schools have been charged with helping children learn, address the challenges they face, and contribute to our society constructively. We also understand that failure is a part of success and that children require positive relationships with teachers, peers, and other mentors.

The fog of statistics, conflicting data, and the focus on metrics has obscured our vision from what an education is and what schools should be. The fog works to the advantage of corporate and political interests and profit garnered through emphasis on standardized testing, the publication of test materials, and the application of technology. Mandates drive many changes, which direct the flow of money. Special interests push for the market and privatization to drive education. Rather than clearing the haze, the media are complicit in increasing the fog.

Robert McNamara acknowledged that there were lessons to be learned after the Vietnam War. Pushing statistical analysis and promoting the influence of the educational-industrial complex harkens back to McNamara's "Whiz Kid" era. Just like McNamara's experience, there are lessons to be learned from the movement to reform education.

LESSON 1: QUESTION THE ASSUMPTIONS BEHIND POLICY AND DECISIONS

The assumption is that metrics and the market are the roads to quality education. The market, not the common good, is seen as the motivating force that propels excellence and innovation. Choice, vouchers, charters, and for-profit schools are based on a market mentality.

We must ask the following questions:

- What are the assumptions about what an education is and should be in school reform proposals?
- What are the assumptions underlying why markets will make better schools?
- What are the assumptions behind the move to privatize education?
- What are the assumptions behind tests as a measure of educational achievement and progress?
- What are the assumptions behind what a good school is?
- What are the assumptions behind what a good teacher is?
- What are the assumptions behind evaluating principals?
- What are the assumptions behind the criticisms of public education?
- What are the assumptions behind the support from corporate, special interests, or foundations for the reform of education?
- What are the assumptions behind the role of public education in our society?
- What are the assumptions behind state and federal mandates?

Other questions should be raised. If the assumptions are wrong or biased, then the reforms can have a devastating effect on education and our society and must be challenged.

LESSON 2: SKEPTICISM IS A GOOD THING

Research, data, and media presentations must be viewed skeptically to ensure sound statistical procedures and standards. Because something is labeled "research" doesn't make it true. Research can be deceptive and biased. The media, corporations, and foundations present data and research as the hard truth. Skeptics, however, do not drink the proverbial Kool-Aid.

The quote attributed to Mark Twain, "figures don't lie, but liars figure," may not be exactly accurate or broad enough. Figures can lie if they are conceived through inappropriate means, deceitful methods, or if they are reported inappropriately. We all know marketing's use of questionable if not outright devious proclamations through statistics and so-called research. In fact, some large corporations help fund research and use the aura of "objective" professors to highlight their products' success or safety.

Some charter schools report better results than public schools, but they don't always have a comparable cross-section of students to those in public schools. Comparisons between charters and public schools are not always accurate because the samples of students aren't comparable. Some charters screen students, and counseled out—"got to go"—lists exist of students to be pushed out. This creates a false comparison.

Ethics and integrity in reporting data can become the victim of self-interest. Data can be important if they are collected, analyzed, and interpreted correctly and ethically. Otherwise, they are deceptive and destructive.

Skeptics look at data and research and do the following:[1]

- check the arithmetic;
- beware of selectivity in data;
- make sure that when comparisons are made, the groups are comparable;
- check that rhetoric and numbers match;

- ensure the group remains comparable when comparisons are made over time;
- recognize that rising standardized test scores does not necessarily mean rising achievement; and
- check that tests are valid and reliable and used for what they are designed for and nothing more.

Skeptics are wary of decisions made on the basis of a single test or on one indicator, particularly when it may not accurately determine capability and may result in erroneous judgments. Skeptics examine. Skeptics question. Skeptics challenge. Skeptics speak up and speak out.

LESSON 3: INTANGIBLES ARE POWERFUL

Focusing on what is tangible and measurable is shortsighted and destined to fail. Intangibles are powerful because they come from within people—their heart, values, and principles. In fact, people with dedication and passions overcome the odds and succeed. Love, ideas, values, and other intangibles guide our day-to-day lives, as well as in the long term.

Life is not just a batch of statistics or algorithmic projections. People—when faced with issues relating to the welfare of their family, nation, or community—commit to causes based on what is right and good. People who are skilled fail because of the intangibles of integrity, trust, or credibility.

Schools deal with intangibles. Certainly, learning skills and concepts is important, but how they are applied is based on ethics, beliefs, and courage. Great events, including the rise of the United States, took place on the foundation of intangibles—fortitude and resolve.

LESSON 4: QUANTITATIVE ANALYSIS HAS LIMITATIONS

In any human endeavor there are things that cannot be quantified accurately. To think that human beings and learning can be reduced to a simple metric or statistics flies in the face of human behavior. Children's futures cannot be gauged through a test or other statistics because they cannot fully measure the complexity of human beings. Persistence and heart within people overcome many difficulties and failures. Limitations diminish as people move ahead optimistically and with faith in themselves and others.

Assessing human capability and commitment is not a mathematical game. Many examples exist of individuals who got the metrics, passed the tests, got the diplomas, and were declared smart. Wisdom, however, is another matter. Many of the statistical success stories were not able to creatively and honorably traverse life.

Cognitive analysis does not automatically translate into competence and success or moral and ethical conduct. On the other hand, some children who were not successful in school went on to great things because of their character and resolve—for example, Winston Churchill, Thomas Edison, and Eleanor Roosevelt.

Simplistic performance assessment systems divert attention from larger and more complex goals and increase the possibility of corruption and deceit. Growth doesn't always occur in a rational, sequential path. Plans become sterile and ineffective. Statistics focused on short-term results may not be important in the long haul. It's not the speed and miles you travel; it's the destination that matters.

To paraphrase Robert McNamara's quote about war, learning is so complicated that comprehending all the variables is beyond statistical analysis. Each individual child coming to a place called school has a complex genetic, social, emotional, physical, cognitive, and value composition that comes to bear in his or her education and development.

Perhaps it isn't as convoluted as the variables in war, but it's certainly not simplistic or subordinate to statistics, external schedules, or quantitative analysis. Individualized education as an ideal is geared toward working with this complexity, including the intangibles of character and principle.

Unexpected and unplanned events unfold. Surprising forces, invisible to the rational eye, unfurl and change the dynamics. Luck intervenes, unexpected contacts occur, or insight develops intuitively and without regard to plan or expectation. The world is a place in which forces and ideas continue to emerge that were not discernable in strategic analysis and plans.

People have feelings and insights that emanate from their unique life experiences, which can change the thinking and perspectives of others. One courageous or outrageous act can alter perception, thinking, and the best-laid plans. Cause and effect does not work with precision, as unanticipated consequences quake the environment.

Historically, people in the right place at the right time brought about changes that could not have been foreseen. Destiny and creativity, along with a bit of serendipity, alter statistics and outcomes.

Lincoln, for example, who became president after a political career that included losing eight elections and running two failed businesses, achieved beyond what any strategic analysis would have predicted. What would algorithms have predicted? Certainly forecasting that Lincoln would become one of our greatest presidents was not logical or rational at the time.

Here again, the intangibles of persistence and belief could not have been calibrated or controlled. Character and determination can produce great things against the odds. Quantum physics demonstrates that there are unseen forces in the physical world. With human beings that's even more evident as we reflect on our relationships and behavior.

LESSON 5: ETHICS AND WISDOM ARE ESSENTIAL TO BEING EDUCATED AND LIVING A LIFE OF INTEGRITY

School is important, but we have to recognize that education does not stop after graduation. Mastery of content without the understanding of principles and values is not really becoming fully educated. After all, computers can be programmed to regurgitate information and make statistical projections, and they are morally vacant.

Values and a moral sense are prerequisites to living with wisdom. The dilemmas of life require not only a solid understanding of concepts and theories, but also comprehension of and commitment to an ethical framework. Being able to analyze the conundrum of two conflicting positive principles requires wisdom. For example, the issue of security versus privacy is currently being debated. This is a conflict between two positive values in our country and society. Any decision made regarding the conflict between these two principles must be made with understanding and comprehension of the possible outcomes. That takes wisdom.

Learning happens with starts and stops and in spurts. Sometimes we speed through the rapids of insight and comprehension, and at other times it takes the diversion of the quiet and calm alcoves of silent reflection to move to understanding. Learning doesn't follow the hands of a clock.

The issue is not how fast children learn or that learning comes in a sequential and expected timetable. Patience and resolve are necessary to help children continue to persevere and learn in a manner and sequence unique to them. If we communicate to children that they are incapable of learning, then we destine them to not becoming educated to their full capacity.

To think that some children are educable and others are not due to statistics and time line is a grave error. All children should be given the skills to continue to learn. We have a moral obligation not to impede children's perceptions of themselves through shortsighted statistics that may not reflect their real potential.

LESSON 6: PRIVATIZATION OF SCHOOLS COMES WITH RISKS AT THE EXPENSE OF THE COMMON GOOD

Some reformers talk of children and parents as "customers." When you think about it, a mercenary interest exists between owners and customers. Businesses deal with customers for profit. That's the priority. They hope to please their customers so that they make money and the customer returns for more. Sometimes customers aren't presented with all the facts about the product or service. Mercenary interests should not be a factor concerning children's educations.

Privatization and corporatization are geared to profit and self-interest. Education is a large market for test makers like Pearson and other technology companies and instructional materials publishers. We all know from textbook wars and adoptions that when serious money is to be made, content can be compromised. We have experienced the deception of for-profit colleges that made money at the expense of debt-laden students who ended up with little to show for their investment.

Pearson and other corporations have combined with politicians and other groups to get tests mandated and used nationally. Imagine a market that must buy your product because of state or federal mandates.

The old adage, "what gets tested gets taught" is true, particularly when teachers' livelihoods depend on a high stakes outcome.

Wall Street provides the most vivid example. Do parents really want Pearson or other companies to determine what their children should learn? Do people really think that appropriateness and impartiality will dictate what is assessed? These companies certainly will not hold skeptical or critical thinking in high regard as an educational goal. If they did, it might jeopardize their market.

The research on charter schools demonstrates that the market does not increase quality, but it does increase branding and advertising. Corporate or private schools move control and influence away from parents, and such schools are less transparent and accountable than public institutions. When public monies follow corporate or privatized schools, it frequently is directed away from public schools, which must take all children who come to their doors. The public interest can be compromised.

Concerning salaries, some charter school executives make in excess of $400,000, for example, Success Academy, Harlem Children's Zone, KIPP, and Harlem Village Academy.[2] The New York chancellor of education makes approximately $250,000. Curious, isn't it?

In the state of Washington, the state Supreme Court overturned in a 6–1 decision law 1240, the Charter School Act, and declared that charters "devoid of local control from their inception to their daily operation" cannot be classified as "common schools" or have access to "restricted common school funding."[3] Money cannot be diverted from public schools to privately operated charters. Public monies are just that—public transparency is fundamental concerning finance and policies.

In the media, people who have no background in educational research, as teachers, or in other positions in education are pitching educational reform. In what other areas do individuals with no background in the subject become experts in proposing dramatic changes and expenditures?

The common school is a fundamental pillar in our democracy, and to weaken or destroy it leaves children in the hands of corporations or elites with no oversight. Simply because someone has made a tremendous amount of money in technical or entertainment fields does not make him or her an expert on educating children. Celebrity does not equate with competence.

Corporate or special interest values and goals are not necessarily congruent with democracy or the commonweal. They are in the market to make money, raise stock prices, or push a particular political agenda for their advantage. Although all schools face challenges, privatizing education has the dangers of the marketplace at play.

Corporate or foundation control of education does not guarantee transparency or public interest goals. Should public monies go to support private enterprises, the goals and expenditures will not be open to scrutiny as they are with public schools. "Buyer beware" is the moniker of the market. That goes for schools, too.

Privatization of education takes control out of the hands of local citizens. Public education is and was a vital part of our democracy, not simply a means to create workers and job training. There are critical thinking and philosophical goals that are essential, which may not be the goals of privatized programs.

LESSON 7: MANDATES DESTROY CREATIVITY AND INNOVATION

Mandates are powerful and direct attention and behavior. In a time of reform, you would think that freeing creativity and innovation would be a major goal. In education, mandated test metrics and school, teacher, and principal evaluation schemes deaden the ability to pursue imaginative solutions at the local level.

The handcuffs of mandates restrict thinking and energy. The corridor of decision making has been placed in a straitjacket.[4] Mandates direct thinking and arise from powerful forces that individuals feel they are impotent to battle. "Get with the program" is the moniker, and compliance becomes the upshot.

Creative thinkers and new programs cannot blossom in a top-down, mandate-focused organization. The irony is that a major goal of education and our country is creativity and innovation, which are foundations for economic and social success.

LESSON 8: EDUCATION IS MORE THAN TRAINING FOR EMPLOYMENT

Some would have us believe that the sole purpose of going to school is in order to get a job and become employable. Believing that the primary purpose of education is preparation for earning a living is a grave error.

Jobs change over time. Training for today's jobs may be hazardous in the future because they may not exist in the future. A strong general education has a much broader purpose than job training or other utilitarian goals. Getting a job or entering a profession is necessary, but we are more than workers and life is more than a salary.

Being educated is a lifelong process, not a singular event assessed by a grade on a test. An education encompasses the liberal arts, far beyond literacy and basic skills. It incorporates philosophy, art, music, theater, literature, history, and science—all coupled with an understanding of the values, principles, and ethics for life and citizenship.

The facile use of tools of continuing education is part of learning. Technology, for example, is simply a tool. But technology is not an end in itself, and it has hazards and limitations—it's not a panacea. One thing we should understand is that technology changes: it will bring new potential, both good and bad. Optimistic skepticism is necessary when examining any "can't miss" solutions.

LESSON 9: TEACHERS ARE SIGNIFICANT POLESTARS IN STUDENTS' LIVES

Reformers have denigrated teachers and recommend metrics to determine their quality and success. We have all felt the intangibles in relationships, which have had a profound impact on us and were essential in making us who we are today.

Teachers have nourished our souls in dark times of fear and discouragement. They kindled our imagination with insights and challenges. They cared for us when we faced devastating losses or the reality that a dream we had was beyond our reach.

Teachers acted as polestars and challenged us to improve, to do better, and to reach for the stars. They recognized characteristics in us that we didn't see. They told us things in a loving and caring way that we didn't want to hear but needed to recognize. They saved us from our destructive self-concept and encouraged good habits and positive ideas.

Teachers are the real heroes in our lives. They raise us up and teach us by example and passion. They make us understand that we have obligations, purpose, and the ability to live with meaning. They highlight positive values and ethics consistently in small and major ways so that we develop character with integrity and credibility.

Those who disparage teachers and want to measure their ability on the basis of tests do an injustice. They fail to understand that the seeds a teacher plants and their impact may not be evident in one school year, but they continue to blossom and live with us throughout our lives.

LESSON 10: CITIZENS WHO STAND SILENTLY BY WHEN DEMOCRATIC FOUNDATIONS AND THE COMMON GOOD ARE THREATENED BECOME COMPLICIT WITH THE COMPROMISE OF DEMOCRATIC INSTITUTIONS

Public education has a deep and moral connection to local communities and our nation as a whole. The common school was founded on the belief that all citizens should have a right to a free education. Our nation survives and thrives on an educated citizenry. Our destiny rides on the shoulders of our children, who have the obligation to carry forward and live up to the nation's principles and values.

Citizens must examine and question educational proposals and speak out and take political action. Financial interests are powerful, and money talks in state and national politics. Unfortunately, we have seen and experienced that fact. We know how capitalism works, and it doesn't always have the common good as an objective.

Organizing politically and entering the debate locally—or on a statewide and national basis—is our obligation as citizens. The Constitution of the United States reinforces the fact that education of our children should be a local priority and function.

At times we must become outraged and act on behalf of our children against reformers who speak in generalizations and poll-tested language, who have a vested interest financially or politically, or who may desire an education that is not healthy or congruent with our country's principles and values.

Acting locally and becoming involved with public schools is essential, and serving on school boards or committees is important even if you do not have children. Being a steward of public education is a positive way to support local communities.

If we don't stand up, who will—and for what reason or cost? Individuals can make a difference and can mobilize others for noble causes. When it comes to our children, there's nothing more important than creating good schools.

Education is a birthright of all of our children, and it is vitally important in producing not only a smart citizenry, but also, more importantly, a wise one. Louis D. Brandeis, former member of the U.S. Supreme Court, said, "What are American ideals? They are the development of the individual for his own and the common good; the development of the individual through liberty; and the attainment of the common good to democracy and social justice."[5]

Public education provides the foundation for those American ideals. We must support the education of our children for their future and for the common good. The public schools have been and should continue to reach for the ideal of a place called school.

NOTES

1. Gerald W. Bracey, *How to Avoid Being Statistically Snookered* (Portsmouth, NH: Heineman, 2006).

2. Alan Singer, "Big Profits in Not-for-Profit-Charter Schools," *Huffington Post*, April 7, 2014.

3. *Seattle Times*, "State Supreme Court: Charter Schools Are Unconstitutional," September 4, 2015.

4. George A. Goens and Phil Streifer, *Straitjacket: How Overregulation Stifles Creativity and Innovation in Education* (Lanham, MD: Rowman & Littlefield, 2013).

5. Louis D. Brandeis, "Speech on True Americanism," July 5, 1915.

BIBLIOGRAPHY

BOOKS

Adler, Mortimer J. 1941. *Reforming Education: The Opening of the American Mind.* New York: Collier Books.
———. 1997. *Reforming Education: The Opening of the American Mind.* New York: Collier Books.
Barzun, Jacques. 1991. *Begin Here: The Forgotten Conditions of Teaching and Learning.* Chicago: The University of Chicago Press.
Berliner, David, and Gene V. Glass. 2014. *50 Myths and Lies That Threaten America's Public Schools.* New York: Teachers College Press.
Blastland, Michael, and Andrew Dilnot. 2009. *The Numbers Game.* New York: Gotham Books.
Bohm, David. 1994. *Thought As a System.* New York: Routledge.
———. 1996. *On Creativity.* New York: Routledge.
Bolman, Lee G., and Terrence E. Deal. 1995. *Leading with Soul.* San Francisco: Jossey-Bass.
———. 1997. *Reframing Organizations.* San Francisco: Jossey-Bass Publishers.
Botstein, Leon. 1997. *Jefferson's Children: Education and the Promise of American Culture.* New York: Doubleday.
Bracey, Gerald W. 2006. *How to Avoid Being Statistically Snookered.* Portsmouth, NH: Heineman.
Bradley, Bill. 2012. *We Can All Do Better.* New York: Vanguard Press.
Briskin, Alan. 1998. *Stirring of the Soul in the Workplace.* San Francisco: Jossey-Bass Publishers.
Burns, James MacGregor. 1978. *Leadership.* New York: Harper Torchbooks.
Byrne, John A. 1993. *The Whiz Kids.* New York: Currency Doubleday.
Craft, Anna, Howard Gardner, and Guy Claxton, eds. 2008. *Creativity, Wisdom, and Trusteeship.* Thousand Oaks, CA: Corwin Press.
Csikszentmihalyi, Mihaly. 1990. *Flow.* New York: Harper and Row.
———. 1996. *Creativity.* New York: HarperCollins.
———. 2003. *Good Business.* New York: Viking.
de Geus, Arie. 1997. *The Living Company.* Boston: Harvard Business School Press.
Einstein, Albert. 1956. *Out of My Later Years.* New York: Random House.
Goens, George A. 2005. *Soft Leadership for Hard Times.* Lanham, MD: Rowman & Littlefield, 2005.

Goens, George A., and Phil Streifer. 2013. *Straitjacket: How Overregulation Stifles Creativity and Innovation in Education*. Lanham, MD: Rowman & Littlefield.
Handy, Charles. 1989. *The Age of Unreason*. Boston, MA: Harvard Business School Press.
Handy, Charles, and Robert Aitken. 1986. *Understanding Schools As Organizations*. New York: Penguin Books.
Hillman, James. 1997. *The Soul's Code: In Search of Character and Calling*. New York: Warner Books.
Hock, Dee. 1999. *The Birth of the Chaordic Age*. San Francisco: Berrett-Koehler.
Howard, Philip K. 2001. *The Lost Art of Drawing the Line*. New York: Random House.
Isaacs, William. 1999. *Dialogue and the Art of Thinking Together*. New York: Currency.
Kellerman, Barbara. 2004. *Bad Leadership*. Boston: Harvard Business School Press.
———. 2014. *Hard Times: Leadership in America*. Stanford, CA: Stanford Business Books.
Kessler, Rachael. 2000. *The Soul of Education*. Alexandria, VA: Association for Supervision and Curriculum Development.
Kinnard, Douglas. 1979. *The War Managers*. Annapolis, MD: Naval Institute Press.
Kofman, Fred. 2006. *Conscious Business*. Boulder, CO: Sounds True.
Kohn, Alfie. 2004. *What Does It Mean to Be Educated?* Boston: Beacon Press.
Koretz, Daniel. 2008. *Measuring Up: What Educational Testing Really Tells Us*. Cambridge, MA: Harvard University Press.
Kozol, Jonathan. 2007. *Letters to a Young Teacher*. New York: Three Rivers Press.
Leader to Leader Institute. 2004. *Be-Know-Act: Leadership the Army Way*. San Francisco: Jossey-Bass.
McMaster, H. R. 1997. *Dereliction of Duty*. New York: Harper Perennial.
McNamara, Robert. 1995. *In Retrospect: The Tragedy and Lessons of Vietnam*. New York: Times Books.
Mondale, Sarah, and Sara B. Patton. 2001. *School: The Story of American Education*. Boston: Beacon Press.
Nichols, Sharon L., and David C. Berliner. 2007. *Collateral Damage*. Cambridge, MA: Harvard University Press.
O'Brien, William J. 2008. *Character at Work*. New York: Paulist Press.
Parker, Palmer. 1998. *The Courage to Teach*. San Francisco: Jossey-Bass Publishers.
Picciano, Anthony G. 2013. *The Great American Education Industrial Complex*. New York: Routledge.
Pink, Daniel. 2009. *Drive: The Surprising Truth about What Motivates Us*. New York: Riverhead Books.
Ravitch, Diane. 2010. *The Death and Life of the Great American School System*. New York: Basic Books.
———. 2013. *Reign of Error*. New York: Alfred A. Knopf.
Robinson, Ken. 2009. *The Element*. New York: Viking Press.
———. 2011. *Out of Our Minds*. New York: Capstone Publishing.
Rose, Mike. 2009. *Why School: Reclaiming Education for All of Us*. New York: The New Press.
Scharmer, Otto C. 2007. *Theory U: Leading from the Future As It Emerges*. Cambridge, MA: Society for Organizational Learning.
Seife, Charles. 2010. *Proofiness: The Dark Arts of Mathematical Deception*. New York: Viking.
Senge, Peter. 2006. *The Fifth Discipline: The Art & Practice of the Learning Organization*. New York: Doubleday.
Senge, Peter, Nelda Cambron-McCabe, Timothy Lucas, Bryan Smith, Janis Dutton, and Art Kleiner. 2000. *Schools That Learn*. New York: Currency.
Sergiovanni, Thomas. 1990. *Value-Added Leadership*. New York: Harcourt, Brace, Jovanovich.
Shapely, Deborah. 1993. *Promise and Power: The Life and Times of Robert McNamara*. New York: Little Brown.
Vaillant, George E. 2002. *Aging Well*. Boston: Little Brown and Company.

Wheatley, Margaret. 2005. *Finding Our Way: Leadership in Uncertain Times*. San Francisco: Berrett-Koehler.
———. 2006. *Leadership and the New Science*. San Francisco: Berrett-Koehler.
Wheatley, Margaret, and Myron Kellner-Rogers. 1996. *A Simpler Way*. San Francisco: Berrett-Koehler.

PERIODICALS, BLOGS, AND REPORTS

Adams, John. 1785. "U.S. President Letter to John Jebb."
Adams, Scott, John S. Heywood, and Richard Rothstein. 2009. "Teachers, Performance Pay and Accountability." Economic Policy Institute.
Adler, Mortimer J. 1999. "Adler on Education." www.catholiceducation.org/en/education/catholic-contributions/adler-on-education.html .
Anderson, Jenny. 2012, February 19. "States Try to Fix Quirks in Teacher Evaluations." *New York Times*. www.nytimes.com/2012/02/20/education/states-address-problems-with-teacher-evaluations.html?ref=education&_r=0.
Babones, Salvatore. 2015, May 9. "Education 'Reform's' Big Lie." *Salon*.
Berliner, David. 2009. "Poverty and Potential: Out-of-School Factors and School Success." Education Public Interest Center. http://nepc.colorado.edu/publication/poverty-and-potential.
Brandeis, Louis D. 1915, July 5. "Speech on True Americanism."
Carnoy, Martin. 2013, January 28. "What Do International Tests Really Show about U.S. Student Performance?" Economic Policy Institute.
Center on Education Policy. 2007. "Why We Still Need Public Schools." Washington, DC: CEP.
Cuban, Larry. 2014, December 9. "Another Educated Guess about Philanthropy and Reform." https://larrycuban.wordpress.com/2014/12/09/another-educated-guess-about-philanthropy-and-school-reform/.
Cukier, Kenneth, and Vicktor Mayer-Schonberger. 2013, May 31. "The Dictatorship of Data." *MIT Technology Review*, 1.
Davenport, Thomas H. 2009, July 7. "Robert McNamara's Good Brain—and Bad Judgment." *Harvard Business Review*. https://hbr.org/2009/07/robert-s-mcnamaras-good-brain/.
Diedrich, Michael. 2012, January 20. "False Choices: The Economic Argument against Market Driven Education Reform." *Minnesota Policy Institute*, 30.
Economist. 2009, July 9. Obituary. "Robert McNamara, Systems Analyst and Defense Secretary, Died on July 6th, Aged 93."
The 47th Annual PDK/Gallup Poll. 2015, September. *Phi Delta Kappan*. Bloomington, IN: PDK International.
Goudreau, Jenna. 2012, January. "Are Millennials 'Deluded Narcissists'?" *Forbes*.
Handy, Charles. 1991, fall. "The Future of Work in a Changing World." *Aurora*. http://aurora.icaap.org/index.php/aurora/article/view/52/65.
Havel, Vaclav. 1994, July 8. "The New Measure of Man." *New York Times*. A15.
Kantor, Rosabeth Moss. 2011, November. "How Great Companies Think Differently." *Harvard Business Review*.
Malin, Joel R., and Christopher Lubienski. 2015, January 26. "Educational Expertise, Advocacy, and Media Influence." *Education Policy Analysis*, 23(6).
Massachusetts Association of School Committees. 2015, October. "Who Is Being Served." Massachusetts Commonwealth Charter Schools.
Media Matters. 2015, February 23. "New Study Highlights Lack of Education Experts on Point and Online Media." http://mediamatters.org/blog/2015/02/23/new-study-highlights-lack-of-education-experts/202638.
Minow, Martha. 1999. "Reforming School Reform." *Fordham Law Review*, 68(2).

Rosenzweig, Phil. 2010, December. "Robert S. McNamara and the Evolution of Modern Management." *Harvard Business Review*.
Seattle Times. 2015, September 4. "State Supreme Court: Charter Schools Are Unconstitutional."
Singer, Alan. 2014, April 7. "Big Profits in Not-for-Profit-Charter Schools." *Huffington Post*.
Stanford University. 2009. "Multiple Choice: Charter School Performance in 16 States." Center for Research on Education Outcomes. http://credo.stanford.edu/reports/MULTIPLE_CHOICE_EXECUTIVE%20SUMMARY.pdf.
———. 2015. "Center for Research on Education Outcomes Study." http://urbancharters.stanford.edu/news.php.
Strauss, Valerie. 2015, July 26. "Pearson Selling Some Investments to Be '100' Percent Focused on Education." *Washington Post*.
Wallace, Lane. 2009, July 10. "McNamara, Aristotle and the Limits of Analytic Thinking." *The Atlantic*.
Washington Post. 2015, July 1. "Jeb Bush's Education Foundation Releases Donor List a Day after His Tax Returns." www.washingtonpost.com/blogs/post-politics/wp/2015/07/01/jeb-bushs-education-foundation-releases-donor-list-a-day-after-his-tax-returns/.
Wolf, Patrick J. 2012. "The Comprehensive Longitudinal Evaluation of the Milwaukee Parental Choice Programs." School Choice Demonstration Project. University of Arkansas.
Yankelovich, Daniel. 1972. "Corporate Priorities: A Continuing Study of the New Demands in Business." http://schoollibrary.org/articles/McNamara_fallacy.

INDEX

accountability, 4, 32, 37, 79; Bics and broccoli, 80–83; cheating, 7, 34; leadership, 73–77; local boards, 43, 45; stewardship, 48; tests, 87–88; teacher, 30–33, 119; victims, 93–94
Adams, John, 42
Adler, Mortimer, 54, 91, 128
analysis: data analysis, 8, 11; quantitative, 4, 6, 53, 123, 133
analytics, 8, 53
Aristotle, 61, 128
arts: dark arts, 23; fine arts, 64, 71, 104, 111; liberal arts, 64, 67, 142
assumptions: group shift, 21; questioning, 12, 33, 37, 75; reform, 30, 75
avatars, 11, 86

being v. doing, 73–77
Berliner, David, 36
Bics and broccoli. *See* accountability
Bohm, David, 116
Botsein, Leon, 64
Bradley, Bill, 120
Brandeis, Lewis, 144
Broderick, Mary, 48
Burns, James McGregor, 120

carrots and sticks, 34
charter schools, 18–19, 24, 123, 135, 140
common good, 13, 17, 45, 47, 51, 63, 99, 104, 134, 144

conflicts, positive, 75, 114, 115
conscious leadership, 78, 79
creativity: and accountability, 30, 33, 57, 81, 125; and education, 10, 28, 62, 65, 70, 104, 111, 124, 128, 130; and intangibles, 24, 78, 101, 115, 118; and mandates, 29, 38, 141; and relationships, 78, 86, 118, 127
Csikszentmihalyi, Mihaly, 99, 100, 129
curriculum: formal, 67; hidden, 67; liberal arts, 64, 67, 142; training, 67
cyber schools, 131

dark side, reform, 33, 129
data and ethics: analysis, 11; charts and graphs, 24; cherry picking, 23; disestimation, 22, 23; integrity, 20, 135; proofiness, 23
dialogue, 46–47, 51, 115

education v. schooling, 53–54, 57–59
educational triage, 20
ethical pitfalls, groups: group shift, 21; self-deception, 21; self-protection, 21; self-righteousness, 20
ethics, 66, 135, 138; accountability, 119; moral imperative, 81, 109, 110, 112; professional, 21, 120, 121; soul, 102, 103; structure, 22, 112, 121
evaluation: teacher, 7, 30

INDEX

failure, fear of, 33, 125
fine arts. *See* curriculum
flow, 129
Fog of War, 5
Friedman, Milton, 15

Gates, Bill, 14, 17
Goebbels, Joseph, 55–56
goodness: happiness, 130; schools, 9–10, 58, 74; soul, organizational, 100, 102–103, 106
group think, 22

Handy, Charles, 8, 100
happiness, 10, 61, 71, 126, 127–131
Havel, Vaclav, 130
heart, 48, 55, 56, 57, 62, 64, 73, 78–79, 89, 99–102, 105
Hock, Dee, 76, 99

ice cream and murder, 22
integrity. *See* leadership; schools

Jefferson, Thomas, 42

Kofman, Fred, 78

leadership: bad, 75; centralized control, 7; conscious, 78; credibility, 74, 76, 79, 83, 110, 116, 120, 124, 136, 143; cynicism, 75; heart of, 78, 120; intangibles, 24, 28, 74, 79, 86; integrity, 76, 84, 115, 120; listening, 20, 46, 49, 77, 117; military, 76; outrage, 79, 119
Leadership Index Survey, 74
liberal arts. *See* curriculum

Madison Avenue, 13–14, 23, 124
management, scientific, 53
mandates, 15, 17, 33–34, 45–46, 133, 139, 141
Mann, Horace, 3, 8, 43
marketplace, 13, 44, 141; for-profit, 15, 17, 99, 106, 134, 139; privatization, 16–17, 18, 25, 50, 133, 139–141
McNamara, Robert, 3–8, 21, 133, 134; centralized control, 7; *Fog of War*, 5; Ford Motor Company, 4; lessons, 6; quantification, 3; statistical analysis, 5, 27, 134; Vietnam, 3, 4, 5, 7, 11, 126, 134; Whiz Kids, 3, 4, 6, 7, 57
McNamara's fallacy, 5, 11
measurement, 6, 7, 11, 23, 70
media, 7, 14–15, 19, 44, 96, 119, 123, 133, 135, 140
Minnesota Policy Institute: market and schools, 16
moral Issues: moral obligation, 109, 110, 112, 139; moral imperative, 11, 78, 102, 104, 109, 111, 120

No Child Left Behind, 14, 27, 45, 62, 123

O'Brien, William, 56, 99
organizational: culture, 33, 35, 37, 74, 75, 100, 111; soul, 48, 99–103, 106, 124

parents, 9, 17, 31, 36, 42; and local schools, 44, 45, 49, 115, 124, 125; PDK poll, 43, 44; responsibilities, 90, 92–93, 94, 96–98, 98, 128
PDK/Gallup Poll, 43, 44
Pearson Company, 16, 17, 18, 139–140
philosophy: great questions, 48, 58, 89. *See also* wisdom
Pink, Daniel, 34
polestar, 85; leaders, 75; teachers, 71, 90, 142, 143
principals, 33, 47, 49, 134
privatization, 16–18, 25, 50, 139–141
professionals, 21–22, 33, 71, 83, 113
public education: accountability, 45; history, 41–43, 44, 61; principles, 42–43, 44, 45, 47, 51, 61, 120, 143, 144; support, 43–44, 144

quality. *See* accountability

Race to the Top, 27–28, 45, 123
reform : intangibles, 5, 7, 9, 11, 12, 136; integrity,
Rhee, Michelle, 14, 88

school boards: common good, 45, 63, 75; effective, 48–49; principles, 47, 48, 49, 50, 51, 83; stewardship, 48, 50–51; superintendents, 48, 49

INDEX

schools: integrity, 11, 47, 80, 83, 102–103, 110, 111, 112; principles, 42; sanctuaries, 11, 101, 103–106
Schweitzer, Albert, 56
scientific management, 3, 8, 53
Senge, Peter, 79
Sergiovanni, Thomas, 120
significant teachers, 87, 98. *See also* polestars
soul. *See* organization; teachers
special interests, 14, 17, 25
specialness, 95–96
Stevenson, Adlai, 42
stewardship, 48, 50–51
structure and ethics, 111, 112–115, 121

teachers: accountability, 87, 119; evaluation, 30–33; intangibles, 86, 89, 98, 138; soul, 71, 89, 90, 112, 142
testing: accountability, 20, 29, 53, 86, 131; high stakes, 7, 20, 27, 57–58, 62; value-added, 7, 30, 32, 87
thinking: Bohm, David, 116; critical, 10, 28, 141; conceptual, 10, 28, 141; fragmented, 117; group think, 22; skeptical, 18, 28, 58, 63, 91, 135–136
training, 67
Twain, Mark, 135
tyranny of the tangible, 8, 10

unethical action: conduct, 21–22, 35, 75; data, 22, 23, 63
United States Department of Education, 46

Vailliant, George, 55
victims, 92–95

Wall Street, 13, 18, 53, 74, 140
Washington State Supreme Court, 140
Wheatley, Margaret, 118
Whitehurst, David, 31
Whiz Kids. *See* Robert McNamara
wisdom, 3, 8, 9; decisions, 54, 56, 76, 105, 124; education, 55–57, 59, 63, 87, 88, 89, 90, 91, 104, 126, 137, 138

ABOUT THE AUTHOR

George A. Goens, Ph.D. has served at all levels of public education: teacher, principal, director, and superintendent. In Wisconsin, he was superintendent of schools for two districts. He was founding and senior partner of Goens/Esparo LLC, a leadership development and search firm in New England.

He also served as an associate professor in the doctoral program in educational leadership and presented at the national American Association of School Administrators, Association for Supervision and Curriculum Development, and National Staff Development Council conferences on leadership, change, and reform. He authored or coauthored seven books and published more than 60 articles on supervision, change, and leadership. In addition, he designed two charter schools for urban youth in Milwaukee and was an associate with the Connecticut Association of Public School Superintendents.

One of his most important responsibilities—and a primary motivation for writing this book—is as grandfather to Claire, Luke, Julia, Eddie, Caleb, Callan, and Jack.

www.ingramcontent.com/pod-product-compliance
Lightning Source LLC
Chambersburg PA
CBHW030234240426
43663CB00036B/394